I know better, but I keep trying to extract jo small, easily lost. I know better, but it takes a book like this and a resolve and a practice—a thing I receive and choose and walk in. I know better, but I keep needing to be taught. And what a wise, gentle, and—yes—joyful teacher Heidi is. She neither scolds nor cajoles nor spouts platitudes. Her remedy for broken hearts is no mere pep talk. Rather, out of her own experience of shattering loss and grief and from walking with others who know heartache, she takes us back to the true source of joy and shows us anew how to drink deep its living waters.

MARK BUCHANAN
Award winning author of *David: Rise* and *God Walk*

Fresh Joy is a life-giving and deeply transforming book that presents a radical alternative to our current culture, which breeds and feeds on cynicism, criticism, and fear—toxic negativity that damages and destroys the human spirit.

The stories shared in this well-written book deal honestly with the raw and painful parts of life. Yet woven throughout *Fresh Joy* is amazing biblical truth that digs deep into the inexhaustible love and grace of God, encouraging the reader to sow the seeds of gratitude, which have the power to produce the fruit of joy.

Heidi McLaughlin lives what she writes. *Fresh Joy* is a timely and much-needed book for women today. It articulates a strong challenge to live above the attitudes of our culture and embrace the radical, transforming power of joy.

MARGARET GIBB
Founder and director of *Women Together*, international speaker, award winning author of *Faith Life and Leadership*

Is joy possible or even authentic in the valley of deep grief? In *Fresh Joy*, Heidi McLaughlin shares profound secrets of cultivating joy even in seasons of suffering. You won't find any easy answers here or fluffy phrases, but what you will find is deep authentic teaching on growing joy in adversity. Bravo, Heidi! You've hit it out of the park with this book! I will highly recommend it to many in my circles. It is a treasure!

BECKY HARLING
International speaker and best-selling author of *How to Listen So People Will Talk* and *Psalms for the Anxious Heart*

I've never met a single soul who didn't long for joy. *Fresh Joy* tells you how to grab hold of that which your soul craves. Through honest storytelling and raw struggles, and like a faithful friend guiding you by the hand, Heidi makes joy readily attainable to any and all in need of a fresh dose, a daily cup, or a drop in their darkest hour. This is a must read to be ready for any and every circumstance life will bring.

ERICA WIGGENHORN
Bible teacher and author of *Unexplainable Jesus: Rediscovering the God You Thought You Knew*

Is it possible to lose the love of your life, twice, and still find joy? This is where Heidi McLaughlin found herself after the sudden death of her second dear husband, Jack. In her book *Fresh Joy*, Heidi tenderly points to the divine Source of her joy by beautifully weaving together her courageous journey from heartbreak to healing and the inspiring wisdom of others who have found the same Source. No matter where you find yourself, *Fresh Joy* gives you fresh insight into how to embrace this sweet gift from God and in the process realize a joy that will not only heal your heart but overflow to those around you.

ANN MAINSE
Host of *A Better Us* and author of *Coffee with Him*

Heidi McLaughlin's gentle, caring spirit shines through her well-crafted words in *Fresh Joy*. Her honesty and vulnerability not only made me want to read more; they caused me to delve deeper and sample one helping of "fresh joy" after another.

Heidi doesn't mince words about how shattered and broken she feels, but despite the pain, her love for God resonates throughout this entire book. She never once implies that the reader should get over whatever hardships and heartache gnaw. Instead, she respects and encourages the reader, with reflections and tenderness, to focus on the healing power of the Holy Spirit.

There are life lessons—but they aren't preachy—and real stories that tug at the soul. There are incredible breath-holding moments where I found myself awaiting the presence of God. All we need to do is S.T.O.P., listen, and receive. *Fresh Joy* is a good reminder.

GLYNIS M. BELEC
Freelance writer, author, and inspirational speaker

How do you go on when your world is shattered? Not once, but twice? Heidi McLaughlin writes movingly and honestly about the trauma of losing two husbands through sudden deaths. We all suffer loss and deep disappointment at times, but how do we go on? After a crushing loss, how is it possible to embrace a rich, joy-filled life again?

Heidi's new book, *Fresh Joy*, gives practical, wise comfort. Reading this book is like taking the hand of a friend who—although she has been through the worst—comes alongside you and encourages you to go on. She points you to the God who never fails. She gently encourages the discipline of choosing joy. What a perfect book for our times, when so many are suffering. Thank you, Heidi, for writing a wonderful, life-giving book.

NANCIE CARMICHAEL
Author of *The Unexpected Power of Home*, *Surviving One Bad Year*, and other books

When you meet Heidi McLaughlin, she exudes joy. She is an encourager to so many women around the globe, and yet she's been widowed twice and has faced the brink of despair. In raw honesty, she gives us a close-up and personal view of her struggles, including PTSD. Every step on Heidi's journey leads us all the way to our true source of Joy—Jesus!

Fresh Joy provides practical ways to weave joy and thanksgiving into your daily routine. It is beautifully written and personally scripted with love for her Joy-Giver. I've been encouraged, challenged, and refreshed. I know you will be too!

RUTH COGHILL
Author of WOW Bible Study Series and *Unborn. Untold. True Stories of Abortion and God's Healing Grace*

"The door to the reservoir of joy is found in loving relationships, and we must learn to seek them and drink from them." As I read these words, I hear Heidi's voice, speaking affirmations of truth because she has done what she teaches us to do. *Fresh Joy* will usher you into a renewed encounter with Jesus Christ. I hope you decide to buy this book and another for a sister who needs to know how to turn to God for everything she needs. Because joy, in its fuller, spiritual meaning of expressing God's goodness, involves more. It is a deep-rooted, inspired happiness that is not dependent on our circumstances. And that's what Heidi McLaughlin has experienced for herself and what she freely gives away to us who decide to journey along with her by reading *Fresh Joy*.

SHERYL GIESBRECHT TURNER, ThD
Founder of From Ashes to Beauty, Inc., and author of *It'll Be Okay: Finding God When Doubt Hides the Truth*

No one is more qualified to write this book than Heidi McLaughlin. Her experience of clawing her way back to a joy-filled existence, not once but twice, gives her a perspective found nowhere else. If anyone choosing to read this book thinks it will provide quick or simple steps to recover from life's severe blows, they will be sadly disappointed. Heidi describes an arduous but deeply fulfilling journey back to joy.

Rev. TIM SCHROEDER, DMin
Chaplain for Royal Canadian Mounted Police

Heidi's written a gem filled with practical helps, real-life stories, and biblical truth. She's learned much through suffering, and now she draws from her lessons learned in the hard place to lead readers into a new understanding of how pain coexists with joy. *Fresh Joy* contains a message we all need to hear.

GRACE FOX
Global worker and author of *Finding Hope in Crisis: Devotions to Calm the Chaos*

Loss is all around us, and with it comes disappointment that threatens to catapult us into despair. There are many books on joy, and yet the message of *Fresh Joy* is rare in that it spurs us on to cultivate joy amid hardship. There are no simple formulas or spiritual platitudes within these pages. With raw tenderness, Heidi reveals her story of unfathomable sorrow and gently leads us in how to grow joy in the darkness of our storms. Anyone struggling in a difficult place will find this book to be a companion on their walk of suffering and will take comfort in knowing that they too, like Heidi, can recover from tremendous loss and pain to flourish once again.

CYNTHIA CAVANAUGH
Speaker and award-winning author of *Anchored: Leading Through the Storm*

FRESH JOY

Finding Joy in the Midst of
Loss, Hardship and Suffering

Heidi McLaughlin

FRESH JOY:
FINDING JOY IN THE MIDST OF LOSS, HARDSHIP AND SUFFERING
Copyright ©2020 Heidi McLaughlin
All rights reserved
ISBN 978-1-988928-34-0 Soft Cover
ISBN 978-1-988928-35-7 EPUB

Published by: Castle Quay Books
Burlington, ON, Canada | Jupiter, FL, USA
Tel: (416) 573-3249
E-mail: info@castlequaybooks.com | www.castlequaybooks.com

Edited by Marina Hofman Willard
Cover design and book interior by Burst Impressions
Printed in Canada

CASTLE QUAY BOOKS

Unless otherwise marked, Scripture quotations are taken from Holy Bible, New International Version Copyright ©1973, 1978, 1984, 2011 by Biblica, Inc.® Used by permission. All rights reserved worldwide. • Scripture quotations marked TLB are taken from The Living Bible Paraphrase • Copyright © 1971, 1973 by Tyndale House Foundation. Used by permission of Tyndale House Publishers Inc., Wheaton, Illinois 60188. All rights reserved. • Scripture quotations marked MSG are taken from The Message. Copyright © 1993, 1994, 1995, 1996, 2000, 2001, 2002 by Eugene H. Peterson • Scripture quotations marked NLT are taken from New Living Translation, copyright © 1996, 2004, 2015 by Tyndale House Foundation. Used by permission of Tyndale House Publishers, Inc., Carol Stream, Illinois 60188. All rights reserved.

Library and Archives Canada Cataloguing in Publication
Title: Fresh joy: finding joy in the midst of loss, hardship and suffering / by Heidi McLaughlin.
Names: McLaughlin, Heidi, author.
Identifiers: Canadiana 20200300210 | ISBN 9781988928340 (softcover)
Subjects: LCSH: Joy—Religious aspects—Christianity. | LCSH: Joy. | LCSH: Grief—Religious aspects— Christianity. | LCSH: Grief.
Classification: LCC BV4647.J68 M35 2020 | DDC 248.4—dc23

Heidi uses her passion and gifts of speaking and writing in her ministry called "Heart Connections." You can contact her through her web page: www.heartconnection.ca or write to her at:

Heidi McLaughlin
1529 Chardonnay Place
West Kelowna, British Columbia
V4T 2P9 Canada

To my beloved birth children

Michelle and Donovan

Through all our sorrow and uncertainties, you've been my constant thread of joy.

"May you be filled with Joy." (Col. 1:11)
Thank you for joining me on the journey
to FRESH JOY.
May it fill your heart and put
a smile on your FAITH.

Joyfully,
Heidi M. Caughlin

CONTENTS

FOREWORD

"I'd love a cup of coffee. Would you like one?" The words slipped from my mouth before I could retract them.

Coffee is my love language. The smell of it brings a smile to my lips and makes my heart happy. It's how I communicate with my people, and Heidi is one of my people. We've laughed and cried our way through many of life's ups and downs, but nothing was as earth-shattering as the unexpected death of her second husband, Jack.

I can still recall the message I received from Heidi asking for prayer after Jack collapsed in their kitchen while going for a coffee. And the prayers that followed when it became apparent he would not recover. Heidi's normal changed forever before the first cup was brewed, an experience that made each cup thereafter a painful memory. I could understand her decision to avoid drinking it after all she had experienced.

For most of my life, I have believed that the goal is to run from pain. I reasoned that if I could avoid grief and disappointment, I would be in a perpetual state of joy. I now know I was wrong. Over the past three years, I've watched Heidi navigate a journey no one would choose with a level of courage and grace that surpasses understanding. When given the option to run from the pain, she chose to walk through it.

Since 2014 I have been meeting with Heidi and our friend Sheryl Giesbrecht-Turner via Skype for monthly prayer times. These prayer calls began as a way to support each other in our writing and speaking ministries. They were an opportunity to not feel so alone in a profession where you spend a lot of time alone. Little did we know then how our friendship would be a lifeline to help each other overcome some of life's greatest battles.

From our first tearful prayer time following Jack's death to our call a few days ago, I've watched God heal Heidi's heart. Anxious nights turned into peaceful sleep. Sorrow and confusion turned into purpose and power. Joy found a way to shine forth from the pain. What I now realize is that there's an intricate relationship between pain and joy. There is a sense that they coexist and are independent of each other.

To my delight, Heidi welcomed the offer to enjoy a cup of coffee that day. Sitting across from her at the table, I was proud of my friend. This wasn't just about a cup of coffee; it was about finding her way back to joy.

This joy is not dependent upon external circumstances, feelings, or emotions. No, this is a steadfast joy that exists even when there is sorrow, pain, and disappointment. This joy is not something you step into but something you allow to come forth from within. It lives in the secret place and is released during time in God's presence.

Where are you in the process? Maybe you're experiencing the fear and confusion of having your world turned upside down. Maybe you're in a place of anxiety and restlessness about the future. Perhaps you're sitting right on the edge of a new journey with God that will reveal to you the fullness of who he is in your life. Wherever you find yourself today, it is my prayer that you will trust the process the Holy Spirit uses to lead you to fresh joy.

Dr. Saundra Dalton-Smith

Board-certified internal medicine physician and author of

Sacred Rest: Recover Your Life, Renew Your Energy, Restore Your Sanity

ACKNOWLEDGEMENTS

I knew it was time to write a book on joy while I was in Toronto and my grandson Ryan spurred me on with "Nana, you'll love a cup of flat white coffee. Trust me." Ryan knew I hadn't been able to drink coffee since Jack died, but this exquisitely delicious flat white was the beginning of another step toward healing and joy. That coffee incident is just a snippet of the love and encouragement I've received from my family and friends while writing this book.

I am incredibly honoured to include stories from my daughter Michelle Conley Willms and other wonderful people in my life. Thank you to Shaunie Brown, Candace Giesbrecht, Cindy Keating, Carol Rath, Margaret Gibb, and Cheryl Klippenstein. You were so gracious and eager to support me throughout this labour of love. I smile from ear to ear when I see how your words infuse life and colour into the chapters to allow the reader to grasp a deeper perspective.

Then there are my relentless readers who drove through a fierce winter storm to sit at my table and work through many chapters to give fresh insights and words of wisdom. Thank you, Elisabeth (Elsie) Lewke, Kirstin Wakal, Jo-Ann Hemingway, and Michele Layton, for your outrageously loving support. You took the time to read and to give loving and honest feedback. Thank you.

I can't imagine writing a book without prayer support. My faithful prayer partners Saundra Dalton-Smith and Sheryl Giesbrecht-Turner have been by my side and prayed for this book from conception to reality. My She Café Bible study group, newsletter supporters, sister Brigitte, and numerous other gracious friends often stopped me and said, "Hey, Heidi, I'm praying for you." For an author who sits alone at her computer day after day, there are no sweeter words.

I am so grateful to Larry Willard of Castle Quay Publishing House for believing in me and giving me a contract. A big shout-out to my gracious editor Marina Hofman Willard, graphic designers, and everyone involved with this manuscript. It takes a village to create a book.

Mostly, my heart overflows with gratitude for the inspiration of the Holy Spirit, whose breath is on every page. He created the inspiration and creativity in my heart that became words flowing through my fingertips. Every book I write is an act of worship and praise to God. I thank God for the passion, health, and love that helped me write a book to help people discover fresh joy.

INTRODUCTION
THE GROUNDWORK

For most of my life the smell of freshly brewed coffee wafting through our home pulled me in like a magnet. My husband Jack was always the first one up in the morning to make sure we would start our day with a cup of joy. Soon he would shout out, "Honey, the coffee's ready; we can start our morning devotions." Our life revolved around our cups of coffee, with us happily sipping delicious dark liquid throughout the day. But I had no idea how that delightful pleasure would forever change my life. You see, Jack died while going to the kitchen for his cup of coffee.

Through my deepest pain I've discovered that joy and pain do coexist. How joy is not something we brew up first thing in the morning and sip on all day but already resides within us and needs to be called forth. Joy is the currency of heaven and available to all of us, at any time, and throughout any circumstances. We all need to know this because we all crave joy.

We have an insatiable desire for happiness. We want it, we need it, and we can have it. But let's not go for just happiness, because it's joy we need. Because joy is more than just feeling good. Joy is deeper, richer, long-lasting, and rooted in God and his love for us. Our connection with him opens the reservoir for us to enjoy his unshakable and endless joy.

It's a beautiful thing when we crash, survive, grow stronger, and find joy. But I have to admit that this verse in James 1:2 has always aggravated me: "Consider it pure joy, my brothers and sisters, whenever you face trials of many kinds." This isn't a quote to encourage someone facing adversity.

I know what a trial feels like. Since 1994 I have encountered many tragedies, and they have not been joyful. But I concur with the end of that thought in verse 4: "so that you may be mature and complete, not lacking anything."

Oh, wouldn't we all love to be "not lacking anything"? No matter what life throws at us, we're able to stand strong, like a tall, majestic palm tree with deep roots. Bending and bowing. Not breaking. Staying beautiful and joyful.

Nurturing joy, like building muscles or filling a bank account, doesn't happen by wishing or hoping. It takes intention. When I get up in the morning, I decide what clothes and shoes I'm going to wear. I decide on my jewellery and makeup. I can also choose joy.

A crisis always reveals our ability to become angry and bitter or stay joyful. My first husband, Dick Conley, died two weeks before Christmas in 1994. He collapsed and died of a heart attack while playing the sport he loved and lived for: basketball. When the policeman stood on my doorstep and told me I would have to go to the morgue to identify Dick's body, my world shattered into a million pieces. I couldn't fathom ever feeling happiness again. Ever. At the age of 47 I thought my once happy life was done. Kaput.

Dick's death spiralled my spiritual journey into an unfamiliar desert. Alone and desperate to feel anything other than grief, I needed God to help me find victory and recapture my joy. But God was already on it. He worked in the background, orchestrating my daily life according to his plan and timetable for my life on earth. The story continued to unfold as I met a widower named Jack and fell in love again. God reawakened my soul.

Jack and I were married on a glorious blue-sky summer day in June 1996. With our new blended family and a second chance at love and life, we were determined to celebrate and continually tap into God's unending joy. Our love was deep, rich, and fulfilling as we both desired to love God first and then each other in a way that would enrich our lives and honour God.

My loving journey with Jack ended at noon on November 11, 2016. We had spent the morning watching the Remembrance Day celebrations and, as always, holding hands. We were excited and talked about the plans for our upcoming trip in six days to New York. Often we had planned to take this trip, but something always came up. We were really going this time.

Jack went into the kitchen for a second cup of coffee, dropped to the floor, and stopped breathing. While I did CPR on him, he took his last breath. Within 14 minutes the paramedics arrived and brought back a pulse. Would Jack survive?

In a matter of hours our children and grandchildren flew in from all parts of North America. They left their careers, universities—wherever they were—and came home to be in ICU around Jack's bed. It was five days of bittersweet sorrow. We prayed for healing, but God knew this was Jack's time to go to his heavenly father's home, and on

Tuesday, November 15, Jack was released into God's glory. My pastor and friend, Tim Schroeder, who was at my side through the entire ordeal, said, "Heidi, you loved deeply; you will grieve deeply."

Oh, how I wished his words weren't true, but they were. Again. This time, how would I recapture the refreshing fruit of joy?

This book is filled with my stories and the stories of other people who overcame obstacles. But mostly, this book is about how God gifts us with everything we need to tap into his joy. The Bible says, "In this world you will have trouble. But take heart! I have overcome the world" (John 16:33). As Christians, we know we have the blessed assurance of being in heaven and united with Jesus when we die. But how can we be "overcomers" and still find joy while we're still travelling this broken, tarnished, and hurtful planet?

Through surviving the tragic deaths of both of my beloved husbands I was taught by God how to lean into all the gifts he has given me, to come to a place where I am "complete and lacking nothing" and once again filled with joy.

Now is the time to prepare. You can't expect to withdraw a million dollars out of your bank account if there is no money in the bank. In the same way, you can't expect to have joy if your spiritual tank is empty. Invest in God's gifts while the time is right so that you can build a foundation of joy no matter what trials come your way.

My other books have always credited my beloved Jack as my greatest cheerleader and supporter of my writing. This is the first book without my Jack. I miss the hours sitting on our deck, overlooking the glistening turquoise and blue waters of Okanagan Lake and the rugged mountains, and talking about the thrust of each new chapter. His insights and wisdom always sent me in the right direction, and his opinions were invaluable.

This book was written seeking the guidance and wisdom of the Holy Spirit. I talk to the Holy Spirit the same way I talked to Jack. "Does this make any sense?" "Which Bible story should I use?" "Is this too personal or too abstract? Will the reader get it?" "Help me figure out the next chapter."

I thank God that he speaks to me in different ways: through his words in the Bible, wise people, wonderful books, friends, and even quotes on Facebook. I give all glory and honour to him; without him there would be no book. Without his gifts of the Holy Spirit I would not be experiencing fresh hope, a good future, and sustainable joy.

At the end of each chapter, you will find a place to S.T.O.P. This is where you take your questions and allow the Holy Spirit, through the mind of Christ in you, to help you fulfill your life and find joy in ways you could never imagine.

S.T.O.P.

Ask God a question.

S: Scripture verse. A verse is available for reflection.

T: Thanksgiving. Thank God for what he has the power to accomplish.

O: Observation. What would you like to ask God to do in your life?

P: Prayer. Ask him. I end each chapter praying with you because I am passionate about God fulfilling your life in all aspects.

I may never have met you, but I have encountered women similar to you for the past 28 years. I am passionate about all of you becoming strong and beautiful from the inside out. Strength and beauty are not only relevant when times are good, but they prepare us for times when trouble comes. I know God can do this for you because he is the King of kings and Lord of lords, Creator of all life—including yours. It's time to take hold of the gifts God has already given you. It's time to be an overcomer and embrace joy.

To my beloved Jack: Because of your love, I am forever changed.

1938–2016

SUPERPOWER OF THANKFULNESS
5,000 GIFTS

Gratitude produces deep, abiding joy because we know that God is
working in us, even through difficulties. —Charles Stanley[1]

I laced up my running shoes, grabbed my water bottle and iPhone, and sluggishly headed out for my 5-kilometre walk. There was no bounce in my step on this hot summer day, but I was determined to use this next hour to listen to my pastor's latest sermon. With all my travelling, I had missed yet another church service, and I wanted to stay connected to the church's teaching series.

During my hikes, the landscape was usually breathtaking, but that day I was oblivious to the beauty—all I wanted to do was check "take walk" off my to-do list. Finally, I plugged into my cellphone, and the church service sounds erupted. The worship team opened with "Raise a Hallelujah," and unprompted, my step quickened. I was bouncing. The music and song lyrics injected life, hope, and new energy, and I came alive with praise: my hands were in the air, and I was singing off-key. Tears streamed down my face as my heart overflowed with thanksgiving for the worship songs that opened my eyes and transformed my bland day into one of renewed awe of the majesty and beauty of God's magnificent landscape. I was reminded that praise and thanksgiving invite the presence of God. They have the power to stop the enemy's fiery darts and empower the spirit to rise above the drudgery of life to ignite new possibilities and spark joy—even if they

---

1. Charles F. Stanley, "How Grateful Are You?: Assessing Our Thankfulness," InTouch Ministries blog, November 22, 2015, https://www.intouch.org/read/blog/how-grateful-are-you.

don't change the circumstance or scenery. Our thanksgiving and praise are like drops of water falling into an empty rain barrel to refill it and remind us of the Father's love. They widen our understanding of the grace and freedom in Christ. We expect people, career positions, creative comforts, and adventure to give us joy, but these things mostly leave us gasping for air. We need to cultivate thanksgiving so we can have the pleasure of joy.

THANKFULNESS IS A SUPERPOWER

Ten years prior to Jack's death in November 2016, God taught me the power of thankfulness. On September 12, 2010, six days before Jack and I were scheduled to speak at conferences in three different cities in Poland, Jack was diagnosed with gall bladder cancer. The surgeon's explanation of the grim prognosis shook our world. The half-packed suitcases lying on our bedroom floor were a mocking reminder of how quickly life changes. Then there was the gripping angst of the prospect of becoming a widow for the second time. While Jack and I endured the seemingly endless doctors' visits and wait times for x-rays, MRIs, and surgeon's appointments, I desperately looked for hope and peace in God's Word.

Everywhere I turned in the Bible, I encountered verses on thankfulness. It was as though God illuminated the words and they jumped off the pages. I couldn't get away from them. As I lingered over the verses, they infused me with hope and stirred up new energy.

- "Let your roots grow down into him, and let your lives be built on him. Then your faith will grow strong in the truth you were taught, and you will overflow with thankfulness" (Col. 2:7 NLT.)
- "Since we are receiving a Kingdom that is unshakable, let us be thankful and please God by worshiping him with holy fear and awe" (Heb. 12:28 NLT).
- "Let us come before him with thanksgiving. Let us sing songs of praise to him" (Ps. 95:2 NLT).
- "The LORD is my strength and shield. I trust him with all my heart. He helps me, and my heart is filled with joy. I burst out in songs of thanksgiving" (Ps. 28:7 NLT).

Then the verse that rocked my world was "Rejoice always, pray continually, give thanks in all circumstances; for this is God's will for you in Christ Jesus" (1 Thess. 5:16–18). I'd seen this verse numerous times, but my soul's vision had shifted. The words "for this is God's will for you" shook me to the core, and I knew I needed to dig deeper. When I drill into new biblical territory, I start by studying the main word in the original Greek. "Joyful" is translated from *chairete*. The Greek root is often translated "to rejoice, be glad."

When I'm thankful and I turn my eyes toward Christ to ponder his love and goodness, my soul and my perspective shift to give me a revelation of something bigger than myself. Ellen Vaughn, in her book *Radical Gratitude*, expresses this so well: "It's incredible: The small, compliant human action of saying 'thank you' constantly links us to the awesome Creator of the universe. In the practice of perceiving every part of every day as a gift from Him, we stay connected to Christ … as we thank God for His presents, we remain in His presence."[2]

This new insight was like a clearer pair of glasses, opening my eyes and heart to a hidden secret. My joy would return if I gave thanks. That's all I wanted: simple joy.

With all my heart I believed God's Word to be true, and I cracked the first pages of my new "thankful journal." To keep the concept simple and uncluttered, I numbered my entries and kept them to one line each. In the days after Jack's collapse in the kitchen, during his time in ICU, and in the ensuing dark days around the funeral, I was determined to stay thankful. Here are some of my numbered entries from my thankful journal:

2909. In the midst of ripping pain, I feel peace

2910. Michelle dropped everything and flew in from Florida

2911. Janice and Brendon were here in hours

2915. People who bring coffee or tea

2918. The way my children love me

2919. Reading Jack's prayer journal

2920. People who bring food

2923. Alex hugging me

2924. Laughter in the midst of tears

2929. Tim, who took over all the family responsibilities for the last two weeks

2930. Our matching plaid shirts

2934. Everyone went back home safely

2936. Going on a walk with the boys

2938. Reading hundreds of cards

2942. Making it through my first church service

2946. People who *really* care

On May 6, 2019, I reached journal entry number 5,000. Looking back and reflecting over these words since Jack's death, I was amazed that God's command to be thankful is true: it restored my joy.

Please don't think for a moment that this came easily. For thanksgiving and joy to become a reality, I had to fight against my heart's inclination to linger in pain, worry, and

2. Ellen Vaughn, *Radical Gratitude: Discovering Joy through Everyday Thankfulness* (Grand Rapids: Zondervan, 2005), 27.

feeling lost or alone. It took deliberate choices to stop and number my thankfulness. In fact, it was so hard that three months after Jack's death I crashed into a pit of darkness and was diagnosed with PTSD. There were days when all I could write was "I got out of bed today" or "today I put on some makeup and bought groceries." I concur with David in the psalms: "Hour by hour I place my days in your hand" (Ps. 31:15 MSG). If we want joy, we must fight for it using a powerful tool available to all of us: the superpower of thankfulness.

Thankfulness is a cultivated discipline that comes from the realization that God's boundless grace does not entitle one to his blessing and joy, and it doesn't mean I deserve it. But, as God's adopted daughter and a recipient of God's heavenly blessings, I need to turn to him and say *thank you*.

TAKE CARE OF YOUR HEART

To experience deep joy in any circumstance, we must prepare—by learning and cultivating—our soul for storms. Suffering and storms are normal, so, when these difficult times come, we must be ready. We can't run a successful triathlon or climb Mount Everest unless we train; we won't have a vibrant marriage unless we learn humility, forgiveness, and grace; and we won't have a retirement fund unless we save and invest. When an unexpected storm blows in, how can we tap into deep joy if we haven't invested in deep soul care? Let's explore this further with a story wherein paying attention to details could have averted a huge disaster.

It was a harrowing experience for 1,373 passengers and crew members of the *Viking Sky*, a luxury cruise ship from the Norwegian company Viking Cruise, when it encountered a violent storm. Normally that is not a problem for large cruise ships. But in this case, with waves up to eight metres high smacking the ship, the engines were disabled when they ran out of lubricating oil to keep the engines running. After suffering a power blackout, the *Viking Sky* sent out a mayday call. The Associated Press reported that "passengers [recalled] a large wave crashing through glass doors and knocking people across the floor of an area where they were instructed to gather as a muster point." The waves were too high to evacuate the ship by rescue boats, so five helicopters evacuated 479 passengers, winching up passengers one by one as winds howled in the dark night. After the storm, the ship travelled to a Norwegian port under its own power.[3]

This is a victorious end to a disaster story, but I can't imagine being a passenger on a gorgeous luxury cruise liner tossed around in heavy seas due to engine failure caused by a lack of oil. Wow, all this unnecessary angst and extra cost because someone forgot to check the oil levels. Paying attention to details could have averted a huge disaster.

To prepare for ensuing storms—and they will come—we must have a settled assurance that God is on our side, he is a good God, and he wants us to live out our

---

3. Jan M. Olsen, "Official: Norway cruise ship engines failed from lack of oil," *AP News*, March 27, 2019.

very best life. We must learn to trust his word: "If God is for us, who can be against us?" (Rom. 8:31). In her book *Choose Joy*, Kay Warren simply states,

> When your heart does not see the goodness of God, you're not going to say thank you to him. You're not going to experience joy because you're putting your energy into what you don't have, what you don't like about your life, what you wish was different. You ignore all that God has already done and will continue to do in your life.[4]

The Norwegian luxury ship encountered an avoidable disaster because the crew workers in charge of the engine were unprepared. Inattentiveness leaves us wide open to unnecessary pain.

After my first husband, Dick, died, my friend Darlene and I had a raw conversation about how we learn to cope when disaster strikes. She openly admitted, "Heidi, if something like that ever happens to me, I hope I have the deep faith that you do." Not long after this conversation, her daughter died suddenly while asleep. My friend had not taken the time to nurture her heart and build her faith. She was left bereft, floating aimlessly and helplessly. Too often people tell me, "I really want to read my Bible and learn to pray, but I just don't have the time." My question to you is, When will you have the time? Will you have time after the disaster strikes? To find abiding joy during any circumstance or storm, we must learn to prepare.

Throughout the Bible, the metaphor of oil represents the work of the Holy Spirit and God's power. To get ready for our storms, we must soak ourselves in this oil, and it starts by taking care of the most important aspect of our being—our heart. The Bible tells us, "Above all else, guard your heart, for everything you do flows from it" (Prov. 4:23). Here are six ways to get started:

- Invite the Holy Spirit to inhabit every part of your spirit to help you discern God's truth versus Satan's insidious lies.
- Read the Bible and memorize key verses to be your anchors and reminders of God's goodness when your world falls apart.
- Learn to trust God by communicating with him through prayer.
- Joy is like a muscle we need to exercise. Learn to cultivate a thankful heart. Gratitude produces more emotional energy than any other attitude. Grateful people are the happiest and most content people I know.
- Join a Bible study group and connect to like-minded people who are also on a quest to find spiritual strength and power.
- Study the work of the oil of the Holy Spirit.

4. Kay Warren, *Choose Joy: Because Happiness isn't Enough* (Grand Rapids: Revell, 2012), 235.

Then stand amazed at the unexplainable work of the Holy Spirit, who lives within you to give you power to overcome the difficult seasons in your life. Our awesome God wants to be your helper and to guide you through every storm. It doesn't mean you won't feel excruciating pain, disappointment, rejection, or failure. But it does mean you don't have to walk through the storms alone. You'll have someone interceding for you, strengthening you, giving you hope, and reminding you of your purpose and ability to unleash the beautiful fruit of the spirit—the fruit of joy.

CINDY KEATING:
BAD NEWS BLUES AND CELEBRATING EVERYTHING

Cindy Keating is a friend I meet for coffee every couple of months to share the ups and downs of being an author. When she shared her story of 47 book proposal rejections, I was blown away by the way she handled it. Here are her words:

It was a simple challenge, or so I thought. My theme word for the year had sparked a practical idea for a way for my family and me to celebrate our simple life moments together throughout the year. "We'll light a sparkler," I said. "We'll talk about all the things that happen so we can decide together what to acknowledge as extra special. This will be a good way for us to celebrate the things that are meaningful to each of us in different ways."

"But what kinds of things should we notice?" my eldest asked.

"Anything!" I replied. "We can celebrate how hard you studied for a spelling test. We can celebrate the completion of one of your piano pieces. We can celebrate how kind you were to a friend at school or how respectful you're being to your teacher. It can be anything!" Everyone was on board. I knew it was going to be a great learning opportunity for all of us.

The email opened with "Dear Cindy, I'm sorry to say"—and my heart sank. I closed my computer immediately and didn't even bother reading the rest of the email because I knew what it would say. This was my forty-seventh rejection. All rejection emails were the same, and even though I *thought* I was used to the dismissals, for some reason this one still stung.

As I sat there discouraged, contemplating what to do next, a sparkler flashed through my mind. With God's perfect timing, I knew exactly what to do. I marched upstairs.

"Boys, we're lighting a sparkler for Mommy's book!" I exclaimed.

"What? Are you serious? Has an agent contacted you?" my husband enthusiastically asked.

"Does someone like your book, Mommy?" my youngest squealed as he jumped around the kitchen.

"Good job, Mommy!" my eldest piped in while flinging open the cupboard to find a sparkler. I quieted them and motioned for them to sit down at the kitchen table. Then I proceeded to tell them what had happened. Naturally, my husband was sad for me, but my kids? Their confused expressions were priceless. "You want to *celebrate* your rejection?" they sang in unison. I was second-guessing the idea, but I knew it was a teachable moment too beautiful to ignore.

"Sometimes celebrating the meaningful things in our lives won't always involve happy emotions," I explained. "Mommy's *not happy* she got rejected. In fact, I'm sad that the journey is taking longer than I thought, and I'm realizing how hard the road really is. But I *am happy* that I can come upstairs, tell you guys how I feel, and know that, no matter what any agent says or thinks about me as a writer, you guys will still love and support me. I think that's something worth celebrating, don't you?"

The conversation that followed brought tears to my eyes. This simple challenge, which we started as a family a few short months ago, had suddenly turned into a deeply touching and profoundly moving journey about true joy and the power of celebrating all moments in our lives.

"Okay, I know!" offered my eldest. "We can celebrate how hard you've been working for these agents."

"And we can celebrate how kind and respectful you're being even though your heart is hurting, Mommy," my youngest suggested.

My husband chimed in, "And we can celebrate the profound influence you're having on your boys' lives right now—mine included."

So that's exactly what we celebrated.

We lit four sparklers that day because that's what joy does—it flips discouragement, rejection, sadness, confusion, and heaviness right side up and upside down and graciously offers us a fresh perspective and a whole new way to view and live in the world.[5]

GROW YOUR JOY

After I heard Cindy's story, I was amazed that, 47 rejections later, Cindy was still writing, smiling, and trusting that God would connect her with the right publisher. That's what thankfulness does. It elevates our thoughts to a higher level and takes the stance that, despite what life throws at us, we can choose to stay joyful.

---

5. Used with permission from Cindy Keating.

1. Get rid of stuff. A large part of our present generation is obsessed with shopping and having more. "I'll be happy when I have _____." And so we shop and stockpile, rent off-site containers or storage sheds, and fill and label Tupperware boxes until we lose sight of all we have. But here's the hard news: overabundance robs us of joy. Instead of enjoying our stuff, we become stuff managers. Excess stuff confuses and distracts us, and the more we have, the less we value what we have.

Growing up, I had two pairs of shoes: one pair for school and the other for church. I wonder if other parents also said, as mine did, "Heidi, pick up your feet. Don't scuff your shoes." I still remember the smell of the shoe polish when it was brought out of the cupboard every Saturday to polish our shoes. Today, I have over 50 pairs of shoes, but I probably don't value them as much as I should, because I can always go and buy more. The pleasure of acquisition is fleeting. Soon, the next purchase becomes another piece to dust, to keep track of, or to organize. Overabundance destroys value. We need to get rid of our excess stuff, simplify our life, be thankful, and enjoy what we have.

Kerry and Chris Shook, in their book *One Month to Live*, express that point so clearly: "When we are thankful, we become content and full of the peace that only He can provide. Focusing on how grateful we are for what we have prevents us from becoming bitter and greedy for more."[6]

2. Learn to be content. To grow joy, we must learn to be thankful for what we have in the moment. The apostle Paul endured beatings, shipwrecks, hunger, and spiritual storms while he was in chains for Christ. When he wrote the letter to the Philippians, he wasn't sitting on a beach in Maui, but still he exclaimed, "I know what it is to be in need, and I know what it is to have plenty. I have learned the secret of being content in any and every situation" (Phil. 4:12). Wow. To be content with whatever we have is a learned process. It does not come naturally. But if we're always on the lookout for temporary happiness, we won't find ultimate contentment. Why? Because happiness demands a certain outcome. If I get that man, I win, and I'm happy. If I get that job (or that house, or that car), I'll be happy. We have momentary feelings of pleasure and success when things are going our way. Each time we attain our happiness goal, we raise the bar, because we're never satisfied. We get desensitized to the norm because there is always more.

When we let go of our desire for a particular result we can find joy in the rhythms of everyday life. For example, happiness says, "I will be happy if this meal or project turns out the way I anticipate." But joy says, "I'm enjoying every step in this process. If it turns out great, we'll all enjoy it. If it doesn't, it won't be the end of the world." Joy is not a

---

6. Kerry Shook and Chris Shook, *One Month to Live: Thirty Days to a No-Regrets Life* (Waterbrook Press: Colorado Springs, 2008), 104.

response to an outcome; it is a fruit of the Holy Spirit within us. Joy comes from being connected to our creator. Learning to trust God for the ending to our stories is a huge first step to finding contentment.

Mark Batterson gets right to the point in his book *If*: "Joy is not getting what you want; it's appreciating what you have. And in some cases, it requires wanting less! You've got to find fulfillment in the simple pleasures."[7]

3. Remember the great things. Let's proclaim God's goodness the same way David did: "The LORD has done great things for us, and we are filled with joy" (Ps. 126:3). No matter what our circumstances, if we remember what God has done for us, it changes our perspective.

I facilitate a grief-sharing group, and one of the most difficult topics begs an answer for "why did God let this happen to me?" This question drains the energy and life out of the room. I'm acquainted with raw grief, so I let the participants lament, tell their stories, and express their pain. But it would be unfair and unkind for me to leave them in that vulnerable state. So I gently prod them to remember "the great things God has done for them" in spite of their unanswered and gut-wrenching question. Eventually the silence breaks, and I hear things like

- He had dementia, so I do know it was time for him to go. I'm glad he's now free and healthy.
- My son dealt with depression and was an addict, so perhaps this was God's gift—releasing him from his pain.
- I thank God for the people who surrounded me with love during my darkest hours.

The atmosphere changes dramatically as praise and thanksgiving erupt spontaneously: "I thank God for the colour of the leaves in the parking lot"; "I thank God for this group and the openness to share"; "I thank Barb for offering to bring me a meal"; "I am grateful that I'm able to start cleaning out my husband's closet." The laments turn into longing for healing and hope, and energy returns to the room.

When we stop and give thanks for the good things God has done and raise a hallelujah amid our pain or questions, new hope arises, and joy is right on its heels.

4. Pursue physical joy. I love the way God created each of us. Not only does thankfulness give us fresh joy and energy; it also revives us physically. Here's what Rick Warren says in his book *God's Power to Change Your Life*: "Psychologists say that gratitude is the healthiest emotion. Hans Seyle, the father of stress studies, claimed

---

7. Mark Batterson, *If: Trading Your If Only Regrets for God's What If Possibilities* (Grand Rapids: Baker Books, 2015), 126.

that gratitude produces more emotional energy than any other attitude. Haven't you found it to be true that the people who are the most grateful are the happiest people you know?"[8]

There are amazing benefits of thankfulness, and many of them focus on our physical well-being. According to a 2011 study published in *Applied Psychology: Health and Well-Being*, researchers found that participants fell asleep faster and stayed asleep longer after spending 15 minutes jotting down what they're grateful for in a journal before bedtime. It benefits the heart, boosts your immune system, and protects you from negative emotions. Go ahead—Google "benefits of thankfulness," and your jaw will drop at the significant results.

So, what's stopping you from being thankful and raising a hallelujah amid your unpredictably wonderful life?

I made a commitment to myself that I will choose to be thankful until I take my last breath. Right now, my goal is to reach ten thousand reasons to praise God in the middle of whatever circumstances come my way. Come along and join me on this journey. Thankfulness is the superpower of fresh joy. A grateful heart is a heart that is content and free, and it primes the brain for healing and miracles.

---

8. Rick Warren, *God's Power to Change Your Life* (Grand Rapids: Zondervan, 2006), 76–77.

AND ASK GOD TO MAKE YOU JOYFUL

Ask God, How can I be more thankful?

S—Scripture: "The Lord has done great things for us, and we are filled with joy" (Ps. 126:3).

T—Thanksgiving: Looking back I see how you've cared for me even when I didn't know it. Thank you for the great things you do for me every day in ways I can't even imagine. Thank you for caring for me so deeply and richly.

O—Observation: I've come to see that a huge part of my life is waiting for certain results so I will feel the pleasure of success and happiness. I didn't know that if I let go of the outcomes I could have contentment and joy in spite of how life turns out. I need to raise a hallelujah in the middle of my disappointments, pain, and struggles so that God can do his work to produce the best results.

P—Prayer: God, I really want to become a thankful person and to find contentment and joy in spite of what life throws at me. I never realized that overabundance devalues all that I have, so I ask you to please help me declutter my life. Help me to be content with what I have and find joy through all the gifts you have already blessed me with. You are such a good, good father—help me to focus on all your goodness. I need to stop believing the lies of the enemy that more is better and will make me happier. Guide me into your truth, and unleash the reservoir of heaven to fill me with your joy, which is sustainable and never ending. Thank you. Amen.

GOD'S UPPER STORY
A WINDOW INTO HEAVEN

"Joy does not simply happen to us. We have to choose joy and keep choosing it every day."—Henri J. M. Nouwen (Meditations)

We love stories with a happy ending. How do we find resolution when a love story turns bitterly wrong? Where is our joy when heartfelt prayers for healing come with a resounding "no"? I know we're in the middle of God's love story, and he promises to hear all our prayers. But in our darkest hour when we feel that God has turned his face away, we feel abandoned and rejected. After all, the Bible says, "Yes, ask me for anything in my name, and I will do it!" (John 14:14 NLT).

God answers prayers in mysterious ways. We love miraculous stories of a tumour that vanished, a woman who had struggled with infertility finally giving birth, or breast cancer that didn't return. These are the tales that become legends. But stories of unanswered prayer—not so much. And yet we need to share the stories of these unanswered prayers so we don't feel so alone and abandoned by God.

I do love prayer. I have been a prayer advocate and warrior for over 30 years, especially after the death of my first husband, Dick. I fully believe that God is "a father to the fatherless, a defender of widows" (Ps. 68:5), and he does hear our prayers.

During my first widowhood years, God felt very near and was a tangible presence in my daily routine. I prayed for the simplest and hardest decisions: "God, where is the irrigation shut-off?" "God, show me how to prune these bushes." "God, help me to make decisions about my dad's medical condition." "God, when is the right time to sell my house?" At times it felt like God was right beside me, walking me through the haze and darkness of unchartered territory. God was close, intimate, and trustworthy.

But God drove a nail into my heart when he didn't answer my prayer for my beloved Jack's healing. Within hours of Jack taking his last breath on the kitchen floor and then the paramedics reviving his heartbeat, news of this tragedy spread like a contagious virus. Across Canada, America, and Europe thousands of people prayed and believed for a complete recovery. Our family and friends believed for nothing less. He died five days later.

MORE QUESTIONS THAN ANSWERS

Throughout our marriage, Jack and I witnessed and celebrated many answers to prayers. We believed God for complete healing while going through Jack's dismal prognosis of gall bladder cancer. I recall holding Jack's hand while sitting in the surgeon's office and hearing the surgeon say, "I have to remove Jack's gall bladder and surrounding areas, including his liver. If Jack survives the surgery, he will have one to five years to live." We were stunned with the reality of the news, but we pressed into our faith, believing and trusting God for more than five years.

Throughout the days following that depressing conversation with the surgeon, I was thick in the midst of juggling my career as a controller for two automobile dealerships. Plus I was squeezing in endless hours sitting with Jack in hospital and doctors' waiting rooms. Noticing my distress, my colleagues at the dealership were kind enough to send us an enormous arrangement of potted plants, which included a small palm tree.

Throughout the months and years following Jack's surgery, Jack and I watched our palm tree grow into a lush tall plant. God answered our prayers for complete healing, and a year later we rejoiced as Jack's blood tests showed he was cancer free. Today my palm tree still sits in my dining room, and its luscious leaves are a daily reminder of how we rejoiced over answered prayer.

So why would God answer prayers for healing Jack's cancer and then take him home to heaven through a heart attack? Jack and I were savouring the richest time in our marriage with our children, ministry, and recreation and were honouring God by putting him first in every aspect of our lives. Why would my second husband, as did my first, drop from a heart attack and leave me alone once again?

WINDOW INTO HEAVEN

I know God doesn't answer all my prayers with a resounding "yes." I understand. After all, the Bible clearly warns us, "Here on earth you will have many trials and sorrows" (John 16:33 TLB). I've learned to view prayer as a way to develop a deep companion relationship with God rather than an opportunity to always ask for more. I know prayer is not a five-step formula to get me everything I want. I clearly remember praying, "God, you know I love Jack more than life itself. We're doing your good work here on earth and trying to obey you in all things. Jack's worked so hard to stay strong and healthy, and he's too young to leave me. Why would you take him now?"

Because we're human and fallible there are times when we do let bitterness creep into our soul. But as God-seeking women, we can't allow unanswered prayer to compel us to hit the eject button and declare "I'm out of here; I don't trust God anymore. Prayer doesn't work. God doesn't care, and I will live through the pain in my own strength."

I chose to make a deliberate choice to open the window to heaven and get a glimpse into God's "upper story." This upper story is God's big picture of our personal lives, from beginning to end, while we're walking on this earth. It's the redemptive meta-narrative of God's plan for our lives from a heavenly perspective. In the upper story we find out what God is up to, how he is weaving our story into his unstoppable and unchangeable divine story. God, the author of our lives, is writing a grander blueprint of our lives that will unfold in clarity when we see him face to face. For reasons you and I will never know, God has to say "no" now and then.

I agree with Philip Yancey in his book *Prayer: Does It Make Any Difference?* as he looks at the blessing of unanswered prayer:

> By answering every possible prayer, God would in effect abdicate, turning the world over to us to run. History shows how we have handled the limited power granted to us: we have fought wars, committed genocide, fouled the air and water, destroyed forests, established unjust political systems, concentrated pockets of superfluous wealth and grinding poverty. What if God gave us automatic access to supernatural power? What further havoc might we wreck?[9]

When I began my relationship with Jesus Christ in 1978, I wanted to sing like the people on the worship teams—the ones who ended up recording cassettes and albums and travelling around the country performing at concerts. I asked God to give me a perfect-pitch voice as inspiring and engaging as theirs. It never happened. God's plan was to use my voice for prayer and encouragement and to bring the Good News of Jesus Christ to the nations. Thankfully God gave me a speaking and writing ministry, but over the past 25 years I've had to deal with the disappointment and rejection of many "nos."

It gives me comfort and hope when I apply a heavenly perspective to stories in the Bible of the numerous people who also received a "no."

- The prophet Jeremiah anguished and wept for Judah, for the temple, and for Jerusalem not to be destroyed. Jeremiah cried out, "My grief is beyond

---

9. Philip Yancey, *Prayer: Does It Make Any Difference?* (Grand Rapids: Zondervan, 2006), 228.

healing; my heart is broken. Listen to the weeping of my people; it can be heard all across the land ... I hurt with the hurt of my people. I mourn and am overcome with grief" (Jer. 8:18–19, 21 NLT). Jeremiah devoured God's Word—it was a joy and delight to him. Jeremiah was faithful and obedient to the point of agreeing not to marry. Yet when he cried out for God to save Jerusalem, the answer was "no."

- Elijah, the zealous prophet, was worn out and depressed after the showdown with the 450 prophets of Baal. He ran into the wilderness and sat under a solitary broom tree, praying that he might die. "'I have had enough, LORD,' he said. 'Take my life; I am no better than my ancestors'" (1 Kings 19:4). Again, God's answer was "no."

- The apostle Paul pleaded three times for God to remove the thorn from his flesh. Not only was God's answer "no," but Paul was told, "My grace is sufficient for you, for my power is made perfect in weakness" (2 Cor. 12:9).

- Then there was Jonah, who did not want to go to Nineveh. Job, who wanted to die. Israelite armies who prayed for victory endured humiliating defeats. God answered all of them with a "no."

Instant answers and immediate joy are expected in this present generation. Want to know how many more days until spring? Ask Siri. Want to learn how to make apple roses or to crochet? Find the right YouTube video. Want to know the distance from your house to the conference centre? Pull up Google Maps. With our present technology we feel entitled to get immediate answers for the things we need or want. But God is not our latest guru, Google, or Bible Gateway.

God is clothed in majesty and shrouded in mystery. He is far but yet so near. On the day I can create a flower or tree I will feel justified in questioning him. Until then I will subdue my soul by reflecting on these profound words: "Now we see things imperfectly, like puzzling reflections in a mirror, but then we will see everything with perfect clarity. All that I know now is partial and incomplete, but then I will know everything completely, just as God now knows me completely" (1 Cor. 13:12 NLT).

Isn't this wonderful news? No matter how hard we try, we can't figure out God. Saturating ourselves in these truths compels us to let go of our questions and trust God for the day when we will understand everything.

Every intersection of crisis demands a choice. The worn-out cliché "It will either make you better or bitter" is annoying but true. Will we allow unanswered prayers to harden our hearts or use them to push deeper into God's unfailing love, to grow wiser and experience a more profound sense of joy? Our God of the "upper story," who orchestrates everything to fulfill our very best lives, longs for us to trust him in the good and bad things that come our way.

Trusting God through hardship doesn't mean we suck it up and move on. There is a time for expressing honest grief and deep sorrow. David, the author of many of the psalms and a man after God's own heart, was on the run for his life for 16 years. With honesty and pain he lamented and cried out over and over again:

- "I am exhausted from crying for help; my throat is parched. My eyes are swollen with weeping, waiting for my God to help me" (Ps. 69:3 NLT).
- "Hear my prayer, O Lord! Listen to my cries for help! Don't ignore my tears" (Ps. 39:12 NLT).
- "I pray to you, O Lord, my rock. Do not turn a deaf ear to me. For if you are silent, I might as well give up and die" (Ps. 28:1 NLT).

David's laments echo deep into my soul. But we cannot stop there. As we continue surveying David's tumultuous "lower story," the day-to-day events of his life, we get to see God's heavenly perspective, "the upper story," unfold. Finally, David is crowned king of Judah (2 Sam. 2:4). The "upper story" had always been for David to become king, but in the seemingly long wilderness, David had to trust God and stand strong for his daily victories.

GROW YOUR JOY

Sometimes unanswered prayers change our lives dramatically in ways we didn't choose or ask for. I didn't ask to be a widow a second time. The divorce was not in your agenda. The bankruptcy was never in the blueprint. Your child's disability will never change. It's hard to live with the fallout. The Bible says we are to pray and believe, and I'm sure that's what most of you did. How do we move forward without becoming bitter? How do we gracefully move to joy?

1. Accept your lower story. As painful as it is, we have to accept our "lower story," which is our daily struggle of joy and pain. When Jack died, I had to accept the unfair reality that I was a widow once again. This is our time to lament, cry, get angry, and allow the shock to settle in our soul. Accepting our reality and feelings is the first step to moving forward.

2. Seek goodness. While on the run for over 16 years, David, in the middle of his battles and hardships, chose to praise God and remind himself of God's unfailing love:

- "Weeping may stay for the night, but rejoicing comes in the morning" (Ps. 30:5).
- "The Lord is my strength and my shield; my heart trusts in him, and he helps me. My heart leaps for joy, and with my song I praise him" (Ps. 28:7).

Elisabeth Elliot, who lost her husband on the mission field and faced multiple hardships, said this about our loving God: "To love God is to *love His will*. It is to wait quietly for life to be measured out by the One who knows us through and through. It is to be content with His timing and His wise apportionment."[10]

Our natural tendency is to wallow in anger and self-pity instead of seeking goodness. We need to intentionally go to the source of joy: Jesus, the one who drank the cup of suffering of God's wrath so that you and I can have access to joy. Before Jesus went to the cross, he said, "You have sorrow now, but I will see you again; then you will rejoice, and no one can rob you of that joy" (John 16:22 NLT). Jesus could endure this suffering because he knew that his daddy had eternal joy waiting for him in heaven. You and I also have that joy waiting for us, but because of Christ, we don't have to wait. We can actually have it now.

3. Declare victory. Our words have the power to unfold a future filled with blessings. We always have the choice of defeat or victory. In Deuteronomy 30:19 (NLT) God gives us this choice: "Today I have given you the choice between life and death, between blessings and curses. Now I call on heaven and earth to witness the choice you make. Oh, that you would choose life." Joy emerges and grows when we choose to move forward and declare victory.

4. Seek a heavenly perspective. History's biggest unanswered prayer unleashed the greatest miracles and victory. The night before Jesus went to the cross, he bowed his head and talked to his father with this deeply personal prayer: "My Father! If it is possible, let this cup of suffering be taken away from me. Yet I want your will to be done, not mine" (Matt. 26:39 NLT). God's answer was "no." Jesus had to endure the suffering for you and me.

Like a lamb led to the slaughter, Jesus humbly went to the cross, and he experienced the excruciating pain of nails driven into his hands. He accepted all the sin in the world, past, present, and future, upon himself. He endured this suffering so that the curtain separating us from our heavenly Father would be torn in half, connecting us to the reservoir of heaven and enabling us to enjoy a life of freedom and joy, which includes

- Redemption of our sin
- The fruit of the Holy Spirit
- The mind of Christ
- The privilege to come fearlessly into God's presence through prayer
- The opportunity to ask God for wisdom, which he loves to give
- The guarantee of having the Holy Spirit to guide us into God's truth

---

10. Elisabeth Elliot, "To Offer Thanks Is to Learn Contentment," *The Elisabeth Elliot Newsletter*, November/December 1995, http://www.elisabethelliot.org/newsletters/nov-dec-95.pdf.

- The undeserved blessing of being adopted as God's children into his eternal family
- The joy of being lavished with God's love
- The assurance that we will spend eternity in God's glorious presence
- Unending pleasure of joy

5. Grow good fruit. While we're still sitting here on earth with our unanswered prayers, we can only imagine what our "upper story" looks like. With all my heart I believe that one day we will clearly see the beauty and majesty of all God planned before the foundations of the earth were formed. Today I may not fully understand, but I pray along with the British author John Baillie:

Teach me, O God, to use all the circumstances of my life today to nurture the fruits of the Spirit rather than the fruits of sin.

Let me use disappointment as material for patience;
Let me use success as material for thankfulness;
Let me use anxiety as material for perseverance;
Let me use danger as material for courage;
Let me use criticism as material for learning;
Let me use praise as material for humility;
Let me use pleasures as material for self-control;
Let me use pain as material for endurance.[11]

So I cling to my unanswered prayer as an opportunity for God to intertwine his hope and my sorrow to unleash beauty and joy. "Not my will but yours, Lord." Through this unwanted painful journey God has been at my side helping me endure my new reality. I experience his presence as he heals me through his gracious nature, loving family, and faithful friends. His promises of hope point me toward a place where I will be perfect and complete, needing nothing, face to face with the giver of our fresh joy.

---

11. John Baillie, *A Diary of Private Prayer*, rev. Susanna Wright (New York: Scribner, 2014), 95.

AND ASK GOD TO MAKE YOU JOYFUL

Ask God, What do you want me to learn about unanswered prayer?

S—Scripture: "Yes, ask me for anything in my name, and I will do it!" (John 14:14 NLT).

T—Thanksgiving: Thank you, God, that you want me to know and experience your extravagant, generous, and endless love. Thank you that I can talk to you 24-7, that you hear the cries of my heart and you care enough to listen.

O—Observation: God tells me in the Bible that I can ask him for anything and he will do it. I am human, and I need tangible evidence of answers, and it is hurtful and frustrating when I don't see results. The only way to console myself is by remembering there is another story that I don't understand—an "upper story" that is grander than the one I am living. I know God loves me and wants the best for my life, so I have to trust that his answer is somewhere else.

P—Prayer: Heavenly Father, you know my pain and anguish over unanswered prayer. When I cry out in desperation, I need to know you have an answer. I need a tangible response that I can see and understand. I can't understand how heaven can stay so quiet when thousands of people pray. Help me to trust you when I can't sense or hear you. Bind up my hurt and help me to move forward and know that one day I will understand and see. I declare my love for you, even when I feel lost and alone. Please draw close to me and sustain me with your love until I can move forward with new understanding, courage, and joy. Thank you. Amen.

FULLY ALIVE
REFRAMING THE "IF ONLYS"

"There is no pit so deep, that God's love is not deeper still."
—Corrie ten Boom[12]

If only. These gnawing words express deep regret when we can't muster a U-turn or fashion a "do-over." When I speak on this tough topic at conferences it sucks the energy right out of the room. Regret cuts deep. It holds us hostage and sabotages our minds from fulfilling our God-given potential and best future. Brazenly I tell you that the haunting words of "if only" can in fact turn your life into the greatest freedom and joy you will ever experience. Impossible? No. Let me help you remove that ten-ton boulder off your back and unlock your prison door.

Jack and I had every detail planned for our long anticipated New York adventure to start on November 19, 2016. Finally. For years we'd been planning this trip, but something always came up. This time we booked and paid for an Airbnb near Hell's Kitchen and were excited to see the coveted musical *Hamilton*.

It was November 11, 2016, and after Jack and I watched on TV the Remembrance Day celebrations in Canada's capital city of Ottawa, we both got ready to run some errands and then make split pea and ham soup. Before we got ready to go, Jack had another dizzy spell, and this time he lay down on the couch until it passed. I kneeled beside him, rubbing his forehead, and asked him this haunting question: "Sweetie, do you want me to call an ambulance?" Momentarily he paused, and then he replied, "No,

12. Corrie ten Boom, *The Hiding Place* (Netherlands: Chosen Books, 1971).

don't. If we call an ambulance it will jeopardize our travel insurance for New York next week."

I did not call an ambulance. The dizziness passed, and he got up, had a bite to eat, took a shower, and went into the kitchen for his cup of coffee. Then he dropped and stopped breathing.

It wasn't until three months later while in the middle of PTSD that God gave me the picture of me kneeling beside the couch and asking that simple memorable question "Do you want me to call an ambulance?" Should I have defied Jack's "no" and done it anyway? *If only* I had called an ambulance. Would Jack still be alive today? My *"if only"* started to haunt and paralyze me. Did I cause his death by not calling an ambulance?

Soon I realized this "if only" scenario traumatized me. I was in terrible shape, and I needed help. Big time.

During this season I was part of a prayer team in my home church, training for ministry in hands-on prayer for people in need of prayer counselling. During one of the training sessions the Holy Spirit nudged me. "Heidi, you're the one who needs prayer." With pounding heart I bravely shared my "if only" story. With love, compassion, and deep understanding, my group of friends gathered around me, wrapped me in the Father's love, and prayed for my healing. It felt better for a while, but I knew I was not done. My "if only" was deeply imbedded in my soul. I felt as though I was locked in a dark cave and couldn't escape.

I was imprisoned in this "if only" scene by ruminating in the past and not able to move into my future. Mark Batterson in his book *IF* explains it so well: "At some point, most of us stop living out of imagination and start living out of memory. That's the day we stop creating the future and start repeating the past. That's the day we stop living by faith and start living by logic. That's the day we stop dreaming of *what if* possibilities and end up with *if only* regrets."[13]

We don't want to be held captive with our "if only," but how do we move forward?

THERE'S AN ACCUSER

Being in deep grief or trauma makes us raw and vulnerable. We're weak and open to Satan's insidious lies. Satan is the accuser who wants us to believe we're trapped and makes us wonder, *Did I really cause that? Will I ever get over this? What am I going to do now? Who can I trust with my story and fear? This will haunt me for the rest of my life.*

God assures us of his love and warns us about the accuser. The Bible reminds us, "He is a mighty Savior. He will give you victory. He will rejoice over you in great gladness; he will love you and not accuse you" (Zeph. 3:17 TLB). I needed a reminder that God's power would help me find a way out of my "if only" so I could move into a healthy future.

---

13. Batterson, *If*, 14.

Stasi Eldredge in her book *Defiant Joy* talks about God's faithfulness: "When we remember His faithfulness in the past, it gives us the courage to believe that the One who says He never changes will be faithful in our present situation and in our future."[14] I dug into the Bible, and God gave me the poignantly familiar story of the resurrection of Lazarus to help me find healing and move forward. I needed to die to my "if only" regret and move into my resurrection life.

God doesn't want us stuck in our guilt, shame, and self-condemnation of our self-imposed or actual failures. If we believe we're stuck there, it declares that his death on the cross failed to accomplish our freedom.

RESURRECTION LIFE

Resurrection is not just about Easter Sunday. The more effectively we learn to appropriate the death and resurrection of Christ into our everyday life, the more effectively we'll be able to enjoy a fully alive kind of Sunday every day of the year. Resurrection isn't just about what happens after we die; it's about what happens while we live. Jesus died so we can live freely and lightly, not stuck in the accusations of the enemy and our "if onlys."

STORY OF LAZARUS

Mary and Martha were Lazarus's sisters, who lived in Bethany. It's the same Mary who poured perfume on the Lord and wiped Jesus's feet with her hair. And it's the same Martha who grumbled about working in the kitchen all by herself while her sister lounged at Jesus's feet. Their home was a special haven and a place where Jesus could kick off his sandals and be with his trusted friends. Then Lazarus got sick. They knew of Jesus's miracles of healing and raising people from the dead. So the sisters sent word to Jesus: "Lord, the one you love is sick" (John 11:3).

Jesus loved Martha, Mary, and their brother Lazarus. When he was told that Lazarus was dead he could easily have returned to Bethany to help his friends. After all, he was only two miles from their home, near Jerusalem, preaching beyond the Jordan. But strangely he didn't go back to Bethany to be with Mary and Martha to help them or comfort them. In fact, he stayed in Jerusalem two more days. The sisters must have been shocked and wondering, *Where is Jesus? Why hasn't he come yet? I thought he loved us.* Mary and Martha had seen Jesus do miracles; they knew he could heal their brother.

LOCKED IN THE "IF ONLY"

Jesus arrived, but it was too late. Lazarus was dead. Martha and Mary heard that Jesus was coming to comfort them, and Martha ran out to meet Jesus, but Mary stayed at

14. Stasi Eldredge, *Defiant Joy: Taking Hold of Hope, Beauty, and Life in a Hurting World* (Nashville: Nelson Books, 2018), 167.

home. Hmm, makes me wonder why. Was she too hurt? Was she angry? Was she in such deep in grief that she couldn't move? But Martha, the extrovert, the doer, ran right to her point of pain. "'Lord,' Martha said to Jesus, 'if you had been here, my brother would not have died'" (v. 21).

If … only. Haunting words. Words that express a deep dejection of a loss where you can't fix it. It's done. Can't go back. It's too late. Jesus could have prevented this; why didn't he? How do we move beyond a point of no return?

- If only I had paid more attention, was more insistent.
- If only I hadn't been caught. Said that. Done that.
- If only I had resisted that temptation.
- If only I hadn't started gambling, drinking, overeating.
- If only I had done what you asked me to do.
- If only God made me more beautiful and smarter, gave me better abilities.
- If only I had a husband, I would finally find my joy.

What is your "if only"? We desperately want to turn back the clock, but we're trapped. Jesus doesn't turn back the clock, but he also does not want us locked into our past. He doesn't want us to agonize over the past; he wants to bring us out of our self-imposed prison. He has a plan, and he wants to set us free.

Jesus says, "I am the resurrection and the life" (v. 25). "It's not something that I will eventually do; it's who I am. I am not a set of rules, tradition, or religion. I am your resurrection life. Not just after you die, but right now so you can live."

My friend and mentor Margaret Gibb shares a story of grappling with her "if onlys" during a harsh season of ministry:

Worry engulfed my whole body. Today we would find out if my husband would need to resign from a church where we were called to pastor. With a red pen I circled the date on my calendar and wrote: "This is the day that the Lord has made." I omitted the next part of that verse because I could not "rejoice and be glad in it." Our family was in the middle of a life crisis.

This was not the first time in my life I had fought the toxic power of worry and fear. Those emotions plagued me all my life. I was an insecure child, fearing everything—people, speaking out, rejection, and failure. I lived in the wasteland of "If Only"—"If only I wasn't me!" My call to ministry was real, but my insecurities and inadequacies loomed like a thick dark cloud, blocking the reality of God's promises and love for me. I didn't know how God would or could use me!

When I married a man who also had a call to ministry, I felt safe … temporarily! But still, the "if onlys" knocked on my heart's door many times: "If only we were not in this church. If only I lived closer to my family. If only we had more money to pay our bills."

Determined to gently break the layers of my defeating attitude I saturated my soul with prayer, reading and diving into God's Word. I learned I can trust God's truth, but not the messages in my mind filled with worry, fear and "if onlys!" Feelings are unreliable in matters of faith. During this difficult time in my life I had to reframe my attitude and my circumstances through the light of God's promises.

On one of my daily walks I learned a spiritual lesson that anchored me. Winter was on its way out. Daffodils had broken through the cold stubborn soil. Intently, I looked at this transition in nature with new awareness and the Holy Spirit whispered: "Whenever you go through a death-like experience, there will be a resurrection."

Death-like experience? We were in it. A resurrection? We wanted it. Would it be possible to redeem this life crisis and see something good come out of it?

We did resign and surrendered our grief, thoughts, and feelings "to the obedience of Christ" (2 Cor. 10:5). Daily we chose to see our circumstances from a higher perspective.

Slowly we experienced inner change that turned our worry into worship, our grieving into gratitude, and our sense of failure into marked favour. Our "if onlys" died, and expectancy and new life sprung forth. We were living again by his resurrection life![15]

The ending to Margaret's story is one that we all need. I also desperately needed hope and promises of new life while I was imprisoned in my PTSD. But how would I walk into that pain and walk out free? I thought, *There is part of me that is too far gone, so dead; how can it come to life again?* But hallelujah, I found resurrection life through the rest of the verses of Lazarus's story.

WHERE DID YOU PUT HIM?

Jesus asked only one question: "Where have you laid him?" (v. 34).

Jesus wants to know what is dead in your life. What is causing you shame, anxiety, PTSD, depression, doubt, or fear? What is your lost dream? What happened to your self-worth or the relationship with your husband? How do you get out of this addiction? What is your "if only" place that you think is too far gone with no possibility of new life? Is it buried so deep in your heart that now it's dead and stinky? Jesus wants to know where we've hidden it.

---

15. Used with permission from Margaret Gibb.

COME AND SEE

Here is how resurrection life beings: "Come and see, Lord" (v. 34).

We need to become vulnerable with Jesus and invite him to come and see the deepest part of our pain. We think if we keep it a secret it will be nice and safe. Secrets are never, ever safe. Anything that is hidden in the dark is open territory for the accuser to torment us with hopelessness, condemnation, or shame. As long as we're stuck in the darkness, our spiritual eyes can't see the possibilities of new hope or new beginnings. We need to tell Jesus, "Come and see what is painful and hopeless in my life." Then we need to lead him to that place of pain and tell him what we've buried. We can't allow the accuser to keep us in the grave, wearing our filthy grave clothes.

I had to let Jesus "come and see" my pain. I started the process by stepping into my pain with my trusted friends praying over me. But I knew in my spirit I wasn't done. There was to be more. I needed to find resolution for my guilt and angst for not calling an ambulance. I had to face reality and find truth. This took months of trauma counselling, retelling my story, and trusting God's Word. I found my comfort and hope in several powerful verses:

- "A person's days are determined; you have decreed the number of his months and have set limits he cannot exceed" (Job 14:5).
- "'For my thoughts are not your thoughts, neither are your ways my ways,' declares the LORD. 'As the heavens are higher than the earth, so are my ways higher than your ways and my thoughts than your thoughts'" (Isa. 55:8–9).

I trusted Jesus to help me walk out of my grave of despair, and I felt his compassion and his desire for me to give him my unexplainable pain and story.

JESUS WEPT

Jesus was 100 percent God, and because he was also 100 percent man he understood sorrow and grief. The Bible says, "He was despised and rejected by mankind, a man of suffering, and familiar with pain" (Isa. 53:3). So I knew that Jesus felt pain and had deep love and compassion for me. This gave me strength to face my guilt over not calling an ambulance. "Jesus wept" (v. 35) is the shortest and most empathetic verse in the English Bible. I don't believe Jesus cried over Lazarus's death, because he knew he would raise him from the dead. He wept with empathy for our suffering. With my whole being I believe that Jesus cares enough to weep with me in my caves and sorrows. This compassion spurred me on to begin to face my "if only."

TAKE AWAY THE STONE

Then Jesus said, "Take away the stone" (v. 39).

What you have hidden away and locked up is not hopeless; it needs to be opened up and examined. Jesus wants nothing to block the intimacy and flow of love in your relationship.

We're afraid. We don't want to let Jesus or anyone see the stench, ugliness, or deadness in our life. Rolling the stone away is the final step to receiving resurrection life. Whatever is hidden away, we have to face it and embrace it.

So what does your "if only" look like? If it's guilt you have to identify it, because guilt shows up with two faces, real and false.

False guilt produces condemnation over confessed sin.

Real guilt produces conviction over unconfessed sin.

My guilt, condemnation, and suffering were false. I had not sinned. On several occasions I asked God to forgive me for what I perceived was a mistake. The voice of false guilt and condemnation is Satan doing his dirty deeds to crush our spirits and disorient us from the truth. When I rolled the stone away and looked at the truth, it gave room for God to reveal truth and breathe new life into my parched and weary soul.

However, we also have to look at real guilt. This is guilt over unconfessed sin and a healthy and holy conviction from the Holy Spirit to make us right with God. With an open and repentant heart we need to go to our heavenly Father, confess our sin, and ask the Holy Spirit to help us move into our resurrection reality and new freedom.

FULLY ALIVE

"Jesus called in a loud voice, 'Lazarus, come out!'" (v. 43). Slowly Lazarus walked up from the tomb with his hands, feet, and face still wrapped in strips of linen. Then Jesus said, "Take off the grave clothes and let him go" (v. 44).

For months I wore grave clothes, barely able to eat or sleep. I had lost much weight, and I looked like the walking dead. It was time to embrace all that Jesus had to offer me: resurrection life. Take off my grave clothes. Become fully alive. Ready to once again tap into the fullness of the reservoir of heaven. Fresh joy.

Jesus reaches into the deepest and darkest "if onlys" to take what was dead and breathe unexplainable new life. Jesus had to die to receive his resurrection life. If we give him all the dead and ugly remembrances in our life, he will resurrect them into something new and glorious. Better than before. How? Because Jesus is the resurrection and the life. It's not something he does; it is who he is.

If you believe, this message of hope is for you. The Bible says, "you believe in him and are filled with an inexpressible and glorious joy" (1 Pet. 1:8).

The easy part of being a Christian is getting saved. Even easier is taking in more information and believing Satan's lies and not dealing with the old stuff that is buried away. The hard part is remembering and revealing our "if onlys," recognizing our pain, and telling Jesus, "Come and see."

GROW YOUR JOY

1. Face your bitter sorrow. Our hearts ache, and we know they need fixing. The first step is to run to Jesus, who is the resurrection and new life. We have to accept the death and resurrection of Jesus and die to our "if onlys" because in him we have new life. Stasi Eldredge puts it bluntly: "If we want to live in the power of Jesus' resurrection, we must first pass through the crucifixion. We must stop running … Jesus came to set us free, and in him we can be. But we will not be free if we continue to hide and refuse to face the bitter sorrow that must be braved in order to bear goodness."[16]

Our extrovert friend Martha in the Bible and her grieving friends gave us three simple words: "Come and see." Facing our bitter sorrow and regret is the first step in revealing our feelings so that we can begin healing. Are you ready to say your "if only" out loud, or will you continue to visit the City of Regret with all of its inhabitants year after year? Growing joy doesn't just happen; it takes deliberate and courageous steps.

2. What-if possibilities. I don't want anyone to experience the pain and suffering like I did and get stuck in their "if only." Don't procrastinate; look at all your "what if" possibilities and embrace them. What have you got to lose except gain new and fresh joy?

Joy is a promised inheritance, and it's God's unexplainable gift to you. What if the greatest joy is still out there waiting for you to claim it? I know first-hand that when we heal from the deepest pain, we can experience the deepest joy.

What if you only had one month to live? Kerry and Chris Shook in their book *One Month to Live* make us look at this reality:

> If you knew you had one month to live, your life would be radically transformed. But why do we wait until we're diagnosed with cancer or we lose a loved one to accept this knowledge and allow it to free us? Don't we want all that life has to offer? Don't we want to fulfill the purpose for which we are created? Wouldn't life be a lot more satisfying if we lived this way?[17]

What if God is the God of second chances and wants to turn your "if only" regrets into "what if" possibilities? What if you roll the stone away and your greatest joy is behind that barrier? What if everything you've believed about your situation is a lie

---

16. Eldredge, *Defiant Joy,* 19–20.
17. Shook and Shook, *One Month to Live*, 5.

and God is waiting to reveal His truth? What if your best life is still waiting for you to embrace it?

3. God restores everything. Bones break, and they heal. Houses burn and are rebuilt. God is in the restoration business, especially with our broken hearts. God restored my first marriage and taught my husband and me to love each other even deeper, and our marriage was made even more harmonious. God used my PTSD to restore my soul and make me more empathetic and humble toward other people's stories.

A lady came to me at a conference and lamented that she had an abortion 50 years before and felt that God could never heal her brokenness. She received counselling, and today she is vibrant and helping other women with unwanted pregnancies.

Not only is God in the life restoration business; he makes everything even more vibrant and confident. Not only does God give us new joy; he gives us a deeper, trustworthy joy.

4. Don't forget to be thankful. Being thankful opens the door to possibilities, miracles, and joy. If Jesus the Son of God took time to be thankful, how much more must we aspire to do it? Here are some of my thankful journal entries during the time of my PTSD and healing journey:

3242. Brigitte and Bernie looked after me for 4 days

3245. Shaunie brought supper and sat with me

3250. Being able to pay my bills

3252. Our great Canadian medical system

3253. Listening to snow melting

3268. Beautiful tulips in vases all around my house

3270. Healing prayer with Twyla, Maureen, Brenda, and Shaunie

3277. Laughing with my sister

3293. Michelle came out for a week

3297. Alex washed my deck

3303. Donovan is with me for a whole week

3312. I'm feeling stronger, not so nauseous

3320. A good sleep last night, thank you, Lord

These days my heart explodes with fresh joy. We have to reimagine our "what if" joy through the framework of God's promises and his resurrection power. When we take time to be thankful and remember his faithfulness in the past, it gives us the courage to move into our deepest regrets and reclaim what is ours: joy.

AND ASK GOD TO MAKE YOU JOYFUL

Ask God, Is there a buried "if only" that you want to reveal to me?

S—Scripture: "I am the resurrection and the life" (John 11:25).

T—Thanksgiving: God, I stand amazed that you can take what is dead, restore it, and make it even more meaningful. Thank you that nothing is unredeemable or too stinky for you to breathe new resurrection life into. Thank you that you are so benevolent and approachable.

O—Observation: There are painful things and events in my life that have been hidden, and I've believed them to be safe. I didn't realize that dark secrets and hidden pain give Satan access to bombard me with lies and deceit.

P—Prayer: Heavenly Father, I am amazed that resurrection life is not just for Easter Sunday or when I get to heaven but for every day. Living freely and fully alive with inexpressible joy is what my heart desires. Help me to get there. I ask you to "come and see" that which is dead and buried and help me to remove any barrier standing between you and me. You are the God who moves mountains, and I know you can move any barriers that stand between me and the offer of daily resurrection life. Gently guide me into your truth and power. Thank you. Amen.

JOY GIVERS AND JOY BUSTERS
SIX TRAPS OF A SOLITARY LIFE

"I cannot even imagine where I would be today were it not for that
handful of friends who have given me a heart full of joy. Let's face it;
friends make life a lot more fun." —Charles R. Swindoll[18]

We all need friends—the kind who tell us when we have lipstick on our teeth or a tag hanging out the back of our shirt. Better yet to have friends with whom we spend a balmy summer evening lingering on the patio, watching burning candles, who are vulnerable enough to answer the question "So what has God been doing in your lives in the last while?"

Deep, intimate, and loving friendships that exude joy are life-giving and contagious. God created us for relationship. Not just spiritually but also in vibrant loving face-to-face connections that actually help us to live longer and healthier. Research done by Harvard Medical School says,

> Social connections like these not only give us pleasure, they also influence our long-term health in ways every bit as powerful as adequate sleep, a good diet, and not smoking. Dozens of studies have shown that people who have social support from family, friends, and their community are happier, have fewer health problems, and live longer.[19]

18. Charles R. Swindoll, *Laugh Again, Hope Again* (Nashville: Thomas Nelson, 2010).

19. "The Health Benefits of Strong Relationships," *Harvard Women's Health Watch*, December 2010, updated August 6, 2019.

Wow! Do you want to live a longer, more fulfilling, and joyful life? Then start by building your tribe of "joy givers" through loving relationships with friends or family.

During the spring of 2017, while I was recovering from PTSD, my children left their homes and careers to be my caregivers one week at a time. They cooked for me, took me on walks, drove me to doctor visits, and helped me regain my strength and health. My son Donovan, who is a professor at the University of Las Vegas, Nevada, took the first week in April 2017. Aside from being a professor, he calls himself a "foodie," and his focus was to fatten me up by inspiring me with colourful, inviting, and healthy meals.

"OK, let's get some meat on those bones," Donovan chided. He was determined to help me eat and gain some pounds, as the stress and grief were causing my body to shrink at an alarming rate.

Instead of our usual energetic activities of golfing or hiking, in the evenings Donovan and I sunk into a comfy couch and fixated on Netflix. We found a fascinating series called *Life Below Zero*. Although it was slow moving and sombre, we were both captivated with the show's depiction of the isolated and solitary life in the frozen Artic, with one human motive: survival.

I couldn't fathom living in isolation and surviving the intense cold and unpredictable Arctic storms. Life is tough when it's minus 60 degrees and you're focusing on staying ahead of storms to hunt for food, find shelter, and protect yourself from the hungry and prowling wildlife. Yes, these people have become resilient in physical survival, but how do you become resilient and joyful when you are alone and isolated? Relationships are vital to our soul and shape us from the moment we are born until we die. An article in the *New York Times* gives us uncomfortable information:

> Social isolation is a growing epidemic, one that's increasingly recognized as having dire physical, mental and emotional consequences. Since the 1980s, the percentage of American adults who say they're lonely has doubled from 20 percent to 40 percent.[20]

In fact, in January 2018 the UK appointed Tracey Crouch as Britain's first minister for loneliness to coordinate the government's response to loneliness as a growing public health concern.[21]

WE'RE NOT MEANT TO LIVE IN ISOLATION

We are made in the image of the relationship of the Holy Trinity: God, Jesus, and the Holy Spirit. Throughout the New Testament there are 36 "one-another principles" that

---

20. Dhruv Khullar, "How Social Isolation Is Killing Us," *The New York Times*, December 22, 2016.

21. Tara John, "How the World's First Loneliness Minister Will Tackle 'the Sad Reality of Modern Life,'" *Time*, April 25, 2018.

show us how to nurture and care for one another. We are to love one another, pray for each other, encourage and bless each other, confess our sins to each other, and forgive one another. The Bible says, "so in Christ we, though many, form one body, and each member belongs to all the others" (Rom. 12:5). It's kind of scary to think we "belong" to one another, but the fact remains that our soul nourishment comes from being connected to God and to other human beings.

In his book *Connecting: A Radical New Vision,* author and psychotherapist Larry Crabb opens this vision further by saying, "The central calling of community is to connect, not to disrupt, to release something powerful from within one person into the life of another that calls forth the goodness in another's heart … When times are hard, we need each other most."[22]

We cannot grow into the women God has designed us to be if we are not in tight formation with our different friendship circles. All of us can use the kind of faithful and loyal tribes described in Luke 5:17–19. Picture this: Jesus is teaching in an over-crowded house filled with Pharisees and teachers of the law. "Some men came carrying a paralyzed man on a mat and tried to take him into the house to lay him before Jesus." There is no room, so what do these friends do? They carry the paralytic man up the stairs to the roof, where they take apart as much of the mud and straw as necessary to make a large opening. They lower the mat through the tiles right in front of Jesus, and the paralytic is healed.

Astounding! What joy to have those types of loyal friends! Becoming a joyful woman means taking the time to build life-sustaining relationships in various areas of our life. We have to learn to overcome the traps of believing we can forge through this life as a lone ranger. To cultivate friendship and joy, we have to identify our joy busters: the smoke screen and lies, the isolation traps.

ISOLATION TRAPS

1. Relationships are substantial only when I'm helping to repair someone's life.

This trap jumps out at me like a snake in the bush. During a meeting with a group of Christians our conversation suddenly turned to the topic of how to have deeper relationships. The men squirmed awkwardly, but it was a woman's comment that hurt my heart. This woman explained that as a pastor's wife she devoted her life to helping people repair their lives and ministering to their needs. When one of her children died, she was stunned to discover that none of those people showed up on her doorstep to show kindness or express sympathy. Wow, that stings.

I fell into this trap when I became a Christian and women flocked to me for advice and guidance. It's a powerful ego trip to feel needed. After all, the Bible does say, "Carry

22. Larry Crabb, *Connecting: A Radical New Vision* (Nashville: Word Publishing, 1997, 2005), 131.

each other's burdens, and in this way you will fulfill the law of Christ" (Gal. 6:2). Years later, I recognized that all my advice and hours of sacrifice did not cultivate friendship relationships. I poured out to them, but they poured nothing back. We have to be prepared for this and not be shocked when we end up standing alone.

Ministry is extremely valuable, and all of us are called to do it. But if we're always repairing someone's life, those same people will not necessarily send us Christmas cards or include us in family functions. To avoid this isolation trap we must learn to identify what a ministry relationship looks like. To be aware you're the one pouring into that person's life and not to expect anything in return. Knowing this prevents disappointment or rejection and helps us to focus on relationships that will build a give-and-take friendship.

2. Needing people is a sign of weakness.

When I speak at conferences, often I ask women, "If a sudden adversity showed up in your life, who would you call at two in the morning?" For women, this question is like saying "sic 'em" to a dog rounding up cattle, and it becomes the focus of a weekend discussion. I'm always dismayed to discover how many people don't have anyone they can call at the drop of a dime. In fact, I declare that needing healthy and loving relationships is a sign of strength, because it shows we're smart enough to know we can't make it through life without each other.

Larry Crabb also states, "When we don't connect, we feel empty. We were designed to connect by a connecting God. Anything less leaves us with an awful ache that we mightily wish wasn't there."[23]

After the paramedics came to revive Jack's heartbeat, I needed friends to meet me in the emergency ward to hold me up and pray. My dearest friend, Shaunie, dropped everything, and within minutes I was in her arms. My sister Brigitte was right on her heels. In the next three hours the waiting room in the cardiac unit was filled to overflowing with friends. We hugged, we cried, and then we held hands and prayed. It takes strength to ask for help. We are not meant to suffer and stand alone.

3. Loving and intimate relationships bring pain and disappointment.

The good news is that relationships bring us our greatest joy and fulfillment. It's true. The bad news is that relationships can cause us the greatest pain and disappointments. Our closest relationships are the ones that keep us awake at night when conflict arises. We can spend hours rehearsing hurtful stories, preparing the response dialogue, and trying to understand how this happened. At some time in our lives everyone and everything disappoints or fails us. We live in a broken and sin-filled world.

To become strong we need people we can confide in, and we need supportive people around us to be a shield of protection and love during times of upheaval and crisis.

---

23. Crabb, *Connecting*, 129.

I agree with Larry Crabb when he says, "Connecting is life. Loneliness is the ultimate horror. In connecting with God, we gain life. In connecting with others, we nourish and experience that life as we freely share it."[24]

Jesus modelled communal life for us during the three years he walked and lived with his motley crew of 12 disciples. For three years of 24-7 companionship, Jesus and his disciples ate together, ministered to the needy, and experienced victories of healing and life change, but they also walked through grievous disappointments. Peter denied Jesus. Judas betrayed him. Jesus admitted that he needed his friends when he went to the Garden of Gethsemane and asked Peter, James, and John to pray for him. But Jesus's friends fell asleep when they should have been praying. Thankfully, Jesus knows our inadequacies, and at the end of his life he said, "Father, forgive them, for they do not know what they are doing" (Luke 23:34).

There will always be people in our lives who will hurt us or rub us the wrong way. Kerry and Chris Shook in their book *One Month to Live* illustrate this so well: "The reality is that we're all sandpaper people. We all irritate other people at times, and that's part of God's plan for our lives … They are allowed into our lives for our own good, to smooth away our rough edges and make us more like Christ."[25]

Sandpaper is used on wood to rub away bumps and uneven edges to create a sublime masterpiece. Being scraped and buffed is how we become resilient and how we learn to flourish and find joy even when life is not fair. Yes, it may be less painful to walk through life alone, but think of what you'd be missing without friends. Laughter until mascara is running down your cheeks. Someone listening with his or her heart and validating your feelings. Sharing adventures and building memories. Praying together. Watching a storm or a waterfall. Sitting together at a concert. Enjoying a shared meal.

Why isolate ourselves from something that will bring us the greatest joy we will ever experience? The Bible commands us to accept the people around us in the same way that Jesus accepted his rough and tumble group of 12 disciples. Romans 15:7 says, "Accept one another, then, just as Christ accepted you, in order to bring praise to God." It's a command, not a nice option, because God always knows what we need in order to live our very best life.

4. I don't have time to develop enjoyable and fun relationships.

The essence of God is love, and the most important lesson he wants us to learn is how to love him and one another. Our relationships on earth are preparation for a colourful and glorious family unit that will continue throughout eternity. Let's be honest: we find time for everything that's important to us, like our favourite Netflix series, recreation, social media, or whatever else comes easy and makes us feel good. We must grasp

24. Crabb, *Connecting*, 53.
25. Shook and Shook, *One Month to Live*, 96.

the importance of loving and healthy relationships so that they will jump to the top of our priority list. The Bible is filled with the command to love one another. First John 4:11 says, "Dear friends, since God so loved us, we also ought to love one another."

I agree it takes time and sacrifice to build loving relationships. I love what Rick Warren says in his best-selling book *The Purpose Driven Life*:

> It is not enough just to *say* relationships are important; we must prove it by investing time in them … Relationships take time and effort, and the best way to spell love is "T-I-M-E." … Relationships, not achievements or the acquisition of things, are what matters most in life. So why do we allow our relationships to get the short end of the stick? When our schedules become overloaded, we start skimming relationally, cutting back on giving the time, energy, and attention that loving relationships require. What's most important to God is displaced by what's urgent. Busyness is a real enemy of relationships.[26]

Busyness and daily distractions will not go away, so we need to change our mindset. Relationships became my top priority after my first husband, Dick, died suddenly in 1994. Friends embraced me with practical love by preparing meals, answering phone calls, cleaning my house, driving me around, hugging me, and praying with me. Our priorities shift when our world falls apart. In the middle of tough times we often lose our passion for careers, success, achievements, or accolades. Instead, we need someone beside us who cares, will listen, and will help us to stand strong. "Dear children, let us not love with words or speech but with actions and in truth" (1 John 3:18).

5. I'm self-sufficient; I don't need anyone telling me what to do.

You might agree and say, "It's much easier to live by my rules. That way I don't have to listen to anyone's judgment, criticism, or disapproval. After all, I have Google and social media to help me find solutions to all my problems. I can work from home, do online meetings, and attend online conferences in my comfy clothes." Working from our homes is convenient and a privilege, but we need to make time for hugs and face-to-face connections and to read verbal cues to fulfill the deepest parts of our longings.

There are many positive sides to being self-reliant; it means we don't have to answer to anyone, and when our ideas or projects are successful, we receive all the credit and satisfaction. "Self-sufficient" people can be viewed as feeling secure and content, but there are downsides. People view self-sufficient individuals as strong and can't imagine they might have a problem they can't handle. If we're always in control and have a need to do things our way, over time people will avoid us and we'll find ourselves alone behind

---

26. Rick Warren, *The Purpose Driven Life: What on Earth Am I Here For?* (Grand Rapids: Zondervan, 2002, 2011, 2012), 127, 125.

our walls of self-sufficiency. In fact, never wanting to have anyone tell us what to do is a sign of insecurity.

Thinking they don't need others is a trap insecure people fall into. In Gordon MacDonald's book *A Resilient Life*, the author tackles this insecurity issue by saying,

> Challenge such a person and you are likely to be met with anger, or cries of hurt and offense, or withdrawal. This is a person who cannot stand for anyone to threaten the structure of his or her world, and it is easier to remain aloof and lonely than to enter into the give-and-take that comes when relationships are supple and solid.[27]

We all have gifts and abilities that need to be received and shared so that we all become stronger and wiser. The Bible tells us, "Now you are the body of Christ, and each one of you is a part of it" (1 Cor. 12:27). When we collaborate, we fulfill our lives the way God has wired us to serve him and each other. Look what the Bible says in 1 Peter 4:10: "Each one of you should use whatever gift you have received to serve others, as faithful stewards of God's grace in its various forms."

Growing up we might have heard, "The only person you can rely on is yourself." But ultimately this self-reliance robs us of true love and joy. We need each other to point out our blind spots, encourage one another when life doesn't go as planned, and take time to celebrate our victories. It takes strength to recognize that reliance on others can be healthy and emotionally affirming. So take ownership of the attitude that fostered this false belief and challenge yourself to be vulnerable and work toward a healthy interdependence.

6. Vulnerability in relationships requires me to share areas of my heart I'm not willing to open.

Vulnerability is the key in intimate, healthy, and loving relationships. Vulnerability is the first thing we want to see in others but the last thing we want to reveal about ourselves. Why? Because fear makes us believe that if people know who we are, they will reject us, and we will be left alone in our shame. All of us know the feeling of shame and will do everything to avoid it.

Being vulnerable doesn't mean we spill our guts to everyone we meet. It means being authentic about who we are, when we've messed up, and how we struggle with certain things. We're all fighting battles, and when we open ourselves up to share them, we might be amazed how people respond with grace and understanding.

We're all trying to figure out how to live this complicated and mysterious life. One of the things that stopped me from becoming a Christian until I was 32 was people

---

27. Gordon MacDonald, *A Resilient Life: Finish What You Start, Persevere in Adversity, Push Yourself to Your Potential* (Nashville: Thomas Nelson, 2004), 215, 216.

pretending they were perfect Christians. People who pretend to be perfect turn others away.

After speaking at a conference or weekend retreat, one of the comments I hear most often is "Heidi, thank you for being so authentic and vulnerable." I have experienced enough pain and disappointment in my life that I believe others can benefit from my mistakes. We all need to learn from each other, and the only way we can do this is by unlocking our hearts and sharing experiences.

But we still need to be wise about what we share with our different tribes. When we look to the Bible for wisdom, we see how Jesus models relationships for us. He had his group of 12, but he also had his inner circle of Peter, James, and John, who were with him during crucial and pivotal moments. Two in particular were on a high mountain, one where Jesus was transfigured (Matt. 17:1–11) and the other in the Garden of Gethsemane the night before Jesus went to the cross.

We all need an inner circle where we can be spiritually naked and unashamed. This tribe knows everything about us and loves us still. Building and nurturing this tribe will help us to grow spiritually and become strong. This is the place to share our hopes and dreams, disappointments, yearnings, failures, and questions.

GROW YOUR JOY

To grow joy we need to stand strong, admit our weaknesses, and take time to build our tribes. The door to the reservoir of joy is found in loving relationships, and we must learn to seek them and drink from them. When we connect and share the powerful characteristics of Christ, we experience the fulfillment and joy of what it means to live out the Christian life. The good of every Christian soul is hidden underneath our rubble and shame, and once it is released, we find freedom and a sense of belonging that cannot be found any other way. We help each other go from admitting our "badness" to calling forth each other's "goodness."

After Jack's death, I was intensely grateful for my inner circles. They allowed me to sob, scream, doubt, and struggle with hope. They walked alongside me and infused me with the Father's love and gave me hope through Scripture, prayers, and words of comfort. They sat and listened. They brought food. They hugged and cried. And in my weakness they helped me to stand strong.

To grow joy we have to make relationships our highest priority. They are our "joy givers." We must take the time to build tribes to pray for us, celebrate, grieve, and sandpaper each other to live out our highest calling. This doesn't mean it's easy, but here is how we can start:

- Ask yourself, When you fast forward to the end of your life, what is one sentence you would like people to say about you? Will it include success or relationships?
- Recognize that our greatest accomplishment in this life will be how we loved one another. Love is something that we learn how to do here on earth, and it will be fulfilled in the most glorious way in eternity.
- Ask the Holy Spirit to help you bring out the goodness first in yourself and then in each other.
- Recognize that isolation is a trap the enemy uses so that you are not covered by the protective and loving shield of other Christian friends. Good Christian friends keep us accountable, pray for us, and call us out on things that harm our soul.
- Ask God to fill you with his love and remove any shame so that you can live an authentic and joyful life.

My dear reader friend, trust me when I say, "We must take time and make intentional efforts to build healthy, Christian, loving relationships. They are one of God's greatest gifts to shape us, strengthen us, make us more like Christ, and infuse us with God's dependable joy. At the end of the day, the richest gift we will have is a deep connection with God and each other."

AND ASK GOD TO MAKE YOU JOYFUL

Ask God, What "hard-to-love" person are you asking me to love?

S—Scripture: "Dear friends, since God so loved us, we also ought to love one another" (1 John 4:11–12).

T—Thanksgiving: Thank you, God, that you love me in spite of my weakness and failures. Thank you that you are the essence of love and your son Jesus modelled this for me when he walked on this earth. Thank you that you will help me to love difficult people in my life.

O—Observation: I recognize that to avoid the six traps of a solitary life I need to know how to be in nurturing, loving, and healthy relationships. First, I need to feel secure in my relationship with my heavenly Father and know without a doubt who I am in Christ. Second, I must make the intentional effort to make time to build relationships with others. I recognize that this is how God designed me. Relationships help me to stand strong, but my heart needs to be opened to fully understand all this.

P—Prayer: Thank you, God, that you never give up on me and your love is always there ready to lift me up. Help me to love myself so unconditionally that I will not be afraid to make myself vulnerable to others. I ask you to remove any shame or guilt so that I do not keep protective walls around me. I truly want to have intimate and vulnerable relationships, but it can be scary. I ask the Holy Spirit to reveal any "badness" in my life that I need to deal with so that I can, without fear, enter into authentic relationships with others. Help me to be brave to initiate friendships so that I can build and nurture worthy and necessary tribes that will give me joy and walk with me through times of tribulation. Thank you, God, that you will. I wait with eager anticipation as you and I build relationships together: first with you and then with one another. Amen.

THE JOY SET BEFORE US
MY SILVER LADDER

"No soul that seriously and constantly desires joy will ever miss it.
Those who seek find. To those who knock it is opened."
—C. S. Lewis[28]

I'd known this rickety old ladder intimately for 42 years and always called her "she." When I laid eyes on her in 1977 I saw potential and saved her by the skin of her teeth from being discarded and thrown into a dumpster. In the spring of that year this beat-up rickety paint-splattered ladder became an important part of my family's life.

After I cleaned her up and painted her with two coats of dazzling white, "she" became the focal point of questions and mystique at Christmas. What was her purpose? What was she doing in the middle of the foyer? Covered in evergreens, sparkly ornaments, and pearl garlands, she stood out as the "belle of the Conley house." Year after year she put a smile on my face and evoked magical Christmas joy.

In May 1993 my first husband, Dick Conley, and I moved from Lethbridge, Alberta, to Kelowna, British Columbia, for Dick to start his new position as general manager of a mobile housing plant. By the beginning of December of the following year "she" was adorned with her pearls and glittered in our new big entryway. She was the first one you saw when you walked into our new home. On December 8, Dick went to play his favourite sport—basketball—and he died of a heart attack in the middle of his beloved game.

---

28. C. S. Lewis, *The Great Divorce* (New York: HarperCollins, 2015, originally published in 1945).

Throughout the days preparing for the funeral we ran out of spots to place flowers, so well-meaning friends used the rungs of the ladder for extra space. I was horrified to see her stripped of her Christmas splendour and reduced to a haphazard landing place for funeral flowers. After the funeral I tore the flowers off the steps, ripped off her garland, beautiful decorations, and mini-lights, and stuck her in a corner in my basement. Over the next couple of years I hated Christmas, and I never wanted to lay eyes on her again.

As time passed and after marrying my beloved Jack, it was time to face the reality of reviving Christmas and creating new joyful memories. One day while randomly rummaging in the basement for a shipping box, I saw "she" standing in a corner. Laid bare and stripped of her beauty, she gave me a gut-wrenching reminder of the past dreadful Christmases. It was time to move forward.

I lifted her onto my shoulder and carried her into the garage. I gave her two coats of gold paint, and on her left side I hung fresh garland and mini-lights. Throughout the garland I strung new ornaments depicting joy and music, and I placed her in the middle of Jack's and my new home. For 21 golden Christmas seasons she was once again the "belle of the ball," in the McLaughlin household.

Enter November 2019. This would be my first Christmas celebration in my home since Jack's death, and I needed to make a decision about my ladder. She'd been tucked away in the basement corner since 2016, and it was time to bring her out. With harrowing memories of two deaths and two horrible Christmases I was determined to make the necessary changes to help us recapture Christmas joy. This year both of my children and their families would celebrate Christmas in my home once again. God gave me an idea on how to move forward.

With resolute determination I picked her up and took her into the garage to give her two coats of sparkling silver paint. I placed magnolias, pinecones, and a berry garland along her left side and included twinkling mini-lights. On the top foldout step I placed a poignant picture of Jack and me taken at a Christmas celebration at Sparkling Hills, a hotel near Vernon, British Columbia.

This time "she" displayed a different story, a 42-year narrative of the beauty and pain of refining. Silver is usually obtained as a by-product of the process of purifying other metals, such as copper, lead, and zinc. It is usually separated from its ores using a flotation process and then purified by smelting it at 961.8 degrees Celsius. During the heat and refining process, the silver rises to the top.

THE JOY SET BEFORE US

Christmas 2019, "she" depicted the story of my refining process and how I rose above my painful circumstances. I'd been through the fire and prayed I'd be purified and prepared to once again reflect the joy and love of Christmas. I'd drunk from the cup of suffering far too long. During endless sleepless nights I had cried out, "God, please, please remove this cup of suffering and replace it with new hope, healing, and joy." God heard and answered my prayers. I wanted the world to know that God's promises of healing and hope are real and powerful. Everyone entering my house and beholding my ladder needed to get a glimpse of this Bible verse: "The LORD's promises are pure, like silver refined in a furnace, purified seven times over" (Ps. 12:6 NLT). God's promises are what I've hung on to, knowing that one day I would again experience intense joy. I knew joy was out there for me, but I needed to fix my eyes on Jesus and his promises for me to reclaim it. The writer of Hebrews gave me that hope: "fixing our eyes on Jesus, the pioneer and perfecter of our faith. For the joy set before him he endured the cross" (Heb. 12:2).

Jesus, the Son of God, perfect in every way, was beaten and betrayed and suffered more than I can imagine. In the Garden of Gethsemane, he cried out, "My Father! If it is possible, let this cup of suffering be taken away from me. Yet I want your will to be done, not mine" (Matt. 26:39 NLT). Three times he cried out for his father to take the cup of suffering away, but God did not. Jesus continued down the lonely path of sacrifice because he knew the joy of heaven. Stasi Eldredge in her book *Defiant Joy* captures the essence of this moment so well:

> Hebrews 12 says that it was for the joy that was set before Him that Jesus endured His tortuous death on the cross. But to get to the joy, He first had to be willing to drink the cup of suffering. In the midst of His excruciating pain, Jesus fixed His gaze on His Dad and held on to the joy that He knew was coming to Him on the other side of the cross. He showed us that we, too, can have joy in the midst of our suffering because of the joy that is set before us—and no one can take it away from us.[29]

Whether we like it or not, our suffering causes our faith to be forced out in the open, and it will show its true colours. I visualize anguish to be confusing downward swirly shades of grey and black. When the bottom falls away, there is no energy or room for pretending that life is filled with yellow rays of sunshine.

Pain and trouble are equalizers, and we break just like our neighbours, co-workers, golf partners, or family members. But those of us who are connected to heaven have hope and power to be different. How? Because we have the promise that nothing can separate us from the love of God, and we own the fruit of the spirit called "joy." We're never destitute, because we have something solid and trustworthy to hang on to. We know God will get us through this, and we don't have to put on a phony plastic smile and pretend to be OK.

---

29. Eldredge, *Defiant Joy*, 27.

Even though I'd lost so much weight and looked like I might crash any minute, when people asked how I was doing I always responded, "I'm not so great right now, but I'm going to be OK." Because of the joy set before me I knew silver was on its way. But I also knew it would be a process.

SET FREE IN THE FIRE

Let's be honest; we'll do anything to remove the cup of suffering. We want a quick fix, and it's much easier to erase the pain with alcohol, drugs, another relationship, or retail therapy. I have to admit that for months after Jack's death I depended on Netflix to get me through some nights. I didn't realize how much I needed it until the day a message on the screen told me my subscription was no longer valid. I almost panicked, until I realized the subscription had been paid with a credit card that was cancelled after Jack's death. You've never seen anyone move so fast in calling Netflix in Texas to get me back up and running. I needed that temporary distraction to get me through a temporary crisis. But we can't expect people, adventures, and possessions to make us happy, because God is the only true source of joy. In fact, he's the only one who will be with us as we walk through the fire. The Bible assures us of this: "When you walk through the fire you will not be burned; the flames will not set you ablaze … Do not be afraid, for I am with you" (Isa. 43:2, 5). Now that's awesome and shocking, is it not? Not only will the flames not consume us, they will set us free.

In the book of Daniel there were three young men named Shadrach, Meshach, and Abednego who would not obey the demand of King Nebuchadnezzar to bow down to his ninety-foot gold statue. The king demanded, "Anyone who refuses to obey will immediately be thrown into a blazing furnace" (Dan. 3:6 NLT). The king ordered the strongest men of his army to securely tie up those three disobedient protestors and throw them into a blazing furnace. Did you notice they were tied up? Because when they came out of the furnace they were unscathed, and the only item that burned were the ropes binding them together. The king couldn't believe his eyes and shouted, "Look, I see four men walking around in the fire, unbound and unharmed, and the fourth looks like a son of the gods" (Dan. 3:25).

We need these familiar stories to remind us that we're never alone, that God is always with us, especially when we're walking through the fire.

Another part of the astounding refining process is that it sets us free. Jesus suffered and died on the cross to set us free, and all our suffering is not to be in vain. The power and authority we have through our relationship with Jesus Christ are meant to set us free and become as distinguished and bright as silver. Free from what? It's different for everyone, but for me being set free means the following:

- Drowning out the voices of other people's expectations and listening to God's calling on my life to show me the way. My way and God's way, not theirs.
- Extending grace in grey areas. Prior to my suffering I might have thought, *They should know better. They're not acting like Christians. Why can't they overcome that addiction? Why don't they pray more? How come they're so depressed*? Now I realize everyone is struggling to live their very best life, and for many people it's a daily challenge.
- Not letting offences or people's bad behaviour affect my joy. I'd experienced too much unnecessary pain from thinking people's negative comments were all about me. Often people don't realize what they're saying. All of us say ridiculous things when we're tired or can't make headway with our "to do" list. Mostly it has nothing to do with you or me.
- Stop being fearful. Now I ask myself, "What's the worst thing that can happen to me?" That doesn't mean I live in denial. Simply put, I'm no longer fearful of being alone, unsuccessful, betrayed, sad, or poor. Been there, done that, and I survived to tell about it.

It's not until we hit rock bottom that we wake up and realize that much emotional and spiritual drama is a waste of energy and time. When Jesus walked on this earth he was purposeful and focused but never too busy to spend time with his father. He always made time to show love and compassion to this broken world. He shook off the taunts of the Pharisees and his betrayers and focused on doing the will of his father. He was free from the hooks of this world. He knew of the joy set before him, and his heart pressed him onward. I know that's the Father's will for you and me as well.

TREASURES IN THE DARKNESS

Suffering is not meant to destroy us. I believe that God uses intense suffering to reveal the treasures and wealth that are hidden in the darkness of our sorrows. Until we believe this, we can't trust God to preserve our joy and unleash it once we're ready to move forward. It's hard for us to fathom this truth in the Bible: "And I will give you treasures hidden in the darkness—secret riches. I will do this so you may know that I am the LORD, the God of Israel, the one who calls you by name" (Isa. 45:3 NLT). My reactionary thought on darkness is *The darkness is a lonely place, and I want out of there now. I dislike the dark, dreary days and especially winter solstice. Darkness makes me feel so vulnerable, and I lose hope because I can't see anything.* If Jesus was perfected through his suffering, what makes us think our lives are any different?

We may not see it right now, but there are many treasures in the darkness. Faith is trusting God even when nothing makes sense. The fire and darkness are where our spiritual muscles are developed. Suffering enlarges our hearts so that we can know the Father's love in ways we did not know it before the refining process. When our trust in God grows, we give him permission to use the trash in our lives and turn it into treasures. The same way I turned my trashy ladder into a silver masterpiece, God can take our suffering and darkness and produce treasures we could never imagine.

Will we surrender our cup of suffering and darkness so that God can unleash his greatest treasures in us? Besides the rediscovery of fresh joy, God gave me more treasures. Here are three examples:

- God took me to a deeper level of compassion, empathy, and mercy. While working on this book, I was involved in our church group where we conducted a spiritual gift assessment. Over the years I've done several of these tests, but for the first time one of my top gifts was "mercy." I was shocked and blown away. My gifts have always been pastoring, teaching, exhortation, hospitality, and leadership. Mercy was never at the top of the list. God's character is mercy toward his people, and he requires that of us as well. The Bible tells us, "And what does the Lord require of you? To act justly and to love mercy and to walk humbly with your God" (Mic. 6:8). The world is starved for mercy, and God needs us to act on his behalf. We can't simply muster it up or pretend to have it to impress others. True mercy comes from knowing how fragile we are and that life can change for any of us in a brief moment. Through my journey of darkness God nurtured my spirit of mercy.

- I'm learning to live one day at a time. I'm a planner and visionary and love to know what's happening for the next year. I'm beginning to fully embrace the Bible verse that says, "Therefore do not worry about tomorrow, for tomorrow will worry about itself. Each day has enough trouble of its own" (Matt. 6:34). I'm still a visionary, planner, and list maker, but now my days unfold differently. I hold each day loosely in my hand and commit it to God. My daily prayer is "God, help me to do today what I need to do today. No more or no less. To give glory to your name." I'm learning to surrender my days and let God work them out according to his plans and not mine.

  While writing this chapter, I was looking after grandchildren in the prairies of southern Alberta, and we were in the middle of a huge snowstorm. The schools were closed, and we were stuck at home. Normally I would be thinking, *How long will we be stuck here? What if we need groceries? What will I do with the children all day? What if the power goes out again? What if … what if.* Instead, during those days while stuck at home, we did crafts, baked cookies, played board and card games, and watched funny TV shows.

We had a wonderful time. Hours passed quickly, and we made precious new memories.

• I am more aware of heaven and the "joy set before" me. I'm more passionate about my daily purpose, with eyes fixed on something bigger than myself. The intimacy with my heavenly Father is sure and deep, and I've learned to trust him in the middle of disappointments and setbacks because I know with full assurance that there is a greater joy waiting for me.

Human efforts cannot produce these treasures in the darkness. My precious daughter Michelle has been refined through much suffering during her lifetime, and I see her becoming more beautiful each day. Her cups of suffering include the death of two of her fathers, eight years of dealing with infertility, adoptions that fell through, and now raising a special needs child. Here is her story:

I always wanted the perfect family. A loving husband and two children, a boy and a girl. But life doesn't always turn out the way we imagine, and I never dreamed that not being able to have children would be part of my plan.

When I was 23, my dad died unexpectedly. The intense grief over my dad and discovering I was infertile was almost unbearable. My pain was so raw that I didn't know how to relate to people, and so I isolated myself. I did believe God loved me, and I relied on scriptural verses and worship songs to comfort me. Thankfully we have a close family, and, even though we didn't live close together, we comforted each other as much as we could. After six years of infertility and grief, I began to think that God had forgotten about me. But I was determined to hold on to my faith and that someday God would grant me the desires of my heart.

In 1999, my husband, Tim, and I decided to adopt, and in August 2000 we welcomed our bright-eyed chubby baby boy, Matthew. We adjusted to being new parents and loved being a family of three. I was so grateful to God for answering my prayer and in awe of this miracle of a baby that had been gifted to us by a selfless birth mother. I loved being a mom, and after a few years we began to think about adopting again.

This time the adoption process was a roller coaster of emotions as two birth mothers changed their minds at the last minute and decided to keep their babies. This time my faith was tested like never before. Didn't God love me as much as I thought he did? How could he love me and allow me to suffer like this, not just once but two times? I felt very angry for a while and questioned my faith. I needed answers.

I started reading *Disappointment with God* by Phillip Yancy, and it reminded me of God's love and promises in the midst of a suffering world. We will all have pain and suffering in this world, but God still loves me and is still with me even when I don't feel him. I was reminded that he always wants the best for me and he suffers alongside me.

After our second adoption fell through we received a phone call that another eight-month-pregnant birth mother wanted to give up her baby for adoption. We prayed, and God gave me a peace and faith to adopt our second son, Austin. We felt very blessed and for eight months enjoyed being a family of four. Then unexpectedly I found out I was pregnant! Not only had God blessed us with two children, he was now showing us his love and grace by giving us three. It was more than I had ever asked for or imagined.

Life continues to have its ups and down, and it isn't perfect. Our middle child has ADHD, and daily we struggle and battle with this. But in the uncertainties of life I am finding joy in knowing I am blessed in all that God has done for me. I am saved, I am forgiven, I am loved. I know I can't always see the bigger picture, but I can trust God in knowing this isn't the end of my story. God has so much in store for us when we put our trust and hope in him. Our suffering is only temporary; God's love, joy, and promises are forever.[30]

GROW YOUR JOY

1. From trash to treasure. I'm looking at an ornate fireplace wood rack my granddaughter Mya and I bought at a garage sale in Columbia Falls, Montana. Other items purchased that day were my two-wheeled golf cart and some plants. We thought we'd hit pay dirt. Someone's trash became Mya's and my treasures.

Isn't it exciting that God can turn our trash into treasures? God has treasures available to us, but they aren't found at a garage sale. They are found in the depth of our darkness, sorrow, and pain, and we have to surrender our suffering so he can turn it into something glorious. I love what Kay Warren says in her book *Choose Joy*: "Will I surrender to God in the darkness, believing that I will find treasures of joy, blessing, and meaning here?"[31]

Revealing and acknowledging your suffering is the first step to letting God give you hidden treasures stored in the depths and darkness of your soul.

2. Go for the silver. Maybe someone you love walked out of your relationship. You thought you had the promotion, but once again you were overlooked. Another miscarriage. An adoption fell through again. Divorce papers were served. Don't waste

---

30. Used with permission from Michelle Conley.

31. Warren, *Choose Joy*, 129.

your pain; go for the silver. Don't give up on your life. God is a God of justice, and he knows what you are going through. God never promised us a life without struggle, but he did give us promises of the "joy set before [us]." That's the silver lining in every setback. "And I am certain that God, who began the good work within you, will continue his work until it is finally finished on the day when Christ Jesus returns" (Phil. 1:6 NLT).

The Israelites saw more than a silver lining. After they suffered and were enslaved in Egypt for 430 years, God delivered them. When Pharaoh eventually had a change of heart and let them go, they didn't leave bereft and shameful. The story goes like this: "The LORD caused the Egyptians to look favorably on the Israelites, and they gave the Israelites whatever they asked for. So they stripped Egyptians of their wealth!" (Exod. 12:36 NLT). The Israelites left their enslavement and walked away with wheelbarrows full of treasures. They got the silver lining and more.

That's what God wants to do for you and me, to give us more than we can even imagine.

3. Ask. In the same way that I turned my discarded, beat-up old ladder into a magnificent showpiece, God wants to transform us into a glorious masterpiece. But our human transformation takes more than paint and a glossy appearance; it comes from the Holy Spirit—we "are being transformed into his image with ever-increasing glory, which comes from the Lord, who is the Spirit" (2 Cor. 3:18). Do you see that we can't do this on our own? The ladder couldn't paint itself, and you and I can't transform ourselves. Asking the Holy Spirit to transform us is a moment-by-moment submission. If we want joy we have to ask for it. The Bible tells us to do this: "You haven't done this before. Ask, using my name, and you will receive, and you will have abundant joy" (John 16:24 NLT). It starts by praying, "God, I want to believe you are with me as I walk through the fire. I surrender any lie that says suffering is from the enemy and meant to destroy me. I ask in the name of Jesus that you transform my pain and sorrow into a triumphant treasure. Amen."

The refining process is always painful. Our suffering has to go through the fire in order for beauty and joy to rise to the top. Often we throw out the cliché "every cloud has a silver lining" that was first penned by John Milton in 1634 in his writing called "Comus." This is a colourful depiction of when the sun shines behind a dark cloud; there is an iridescent glow that looks like silver, which means we should never feel hopeless, because every bad situation and suffering has the potential to create something positive and beautiful. When God is the light and the power behind any situation, we are guaranteed brilliant joy.

AND ASK GOD TO MAKE YOU JOYFUL

Ask God, What trash can I give to you to turn into a treasure?

S—Scripture: "And I am certain that God, who began the good work within you, will continue his work until it is finally finished on the day when Christ Jesus returns" (Phil. 1:6 NLT).

T—Thanksgiving: Thank you, God, that when I began my personal relationship with you, you began a good work in me. Thank you for the blessed assurance that you will continue this work until it is finished and perfect.

O—Observation: I forget that God is committed to continue his good work in me. When I go through tough times and drink from the cup of suffering, oftentimes I feel not heard by God; instead I feel alone and abandoned. While I'm going through this I don't realize that in the darkness God is transforming me from glory to glory.

P—Prayer: Heavenly Father, help me to see that while I am in the darkness, you are doing your best work in me. Please instill hope and give me insights of the treasures you are creating in those secret places. Reveal yourself to me in ways I can understand so that I know you are with me as I walk through the fire. Help me to see suffering not as a punishment but as a refining process to get a glimpse of the "joy set before" me. May the pain I'm experiencing create greater passion to know you and to develop a deeper and beautiful intimate relationship with you. Refine me and make me as brilliant and pure as silver. Thank you. Amen.

JOY IN THE DESERT
THE LAND BETWEEN

"All change comes from deepening your understanding of the salvation of Christ and living out the changes that understanding creates in your heart." — Tim Keller[32]

The "land between" is the riptide of transition. You're in the middle of an unknown passageway from one state or place to another, seeking and waiting for your new destination. You've left behind all that's familiar and are moving into the vastness of uncharted new territory. Everything you've ever known is interrupted or has changed. Now you're in a barren landscape of loneliness and unanswered questions, and you're clueless as to how to navigate this new terrain. This shocking transition can happen instantaneously or over time.

The reason can be that you've made a poor choice or lost hope for an unfulfilled dream. It might even be a season in your life when you feel stuck or taken for granted. Or it may simply be the dailyness of life, with no hope of a reprieve. The "land between" might instantly start with a phone call, someone ringing your doorbell, or a horrifying sentence, such as the following:

- Your husband died tonight on the basketball floor.
- Mom and Dad, the adoption fell through again.
- Children, your dad and I are getting a divorce.

32. Tim Keller, *The Prodigal God: Recovering the Heart of the Christian Faith* (New York: Viking, 2008).

- Come and get your child from the police station.
- Your dad just got transferred, and we're moving again.
- There has been an accident.
- Your house is burning.

My "land between" emerged a few hours before midnight going into 1995. On December 15, 1994, I buried my first husband, Dick, and for the next two weeks my house became Grand Central Station with people and activity. With all the bustle and noise I didn't have time to feel alone or to recognize my barren and foreign future. Then, shockingly, one night it showed up. While my daughter Michelle and I were out for a pre-New Year's midnight walk, with razor-blade clarity I entered into my "land between." Strangely enough, this shift happened while I was looking into other people's homes.

With the coal black darkness of the night, the contrast of the light in people's homes made it very easy to see through the windows and watch families preparing New Year's celebrations. I couldn't seem to stop the dialogue in my head as I observed people sitting in their living rooms, at dining room tables, playing games and laughing. *That's what I should be doing right now,* I thought. *I should have my husband and family with me, playing games and making plans for the coming year. We should all be in the kitchen laughing and preparing a New Year's meal. Instead, my daughter and I are out here in the bitter cold, all alone. The past is finished and can't be repeated, and my future is wiped away like a story on a white board. I can't go back, and I don't know how to move forward. I'm in a land between. My joy is gone, and I don't know what to do.*

Quietly and numb with angst for the coming year, I entered this new season as suddenly single and alone. I hated being hurled into a land where now I had to mark status boxes with an X beside "widow." I got married at 19, and after 28 years of marriage I didn't know how to live without either my parents or my husband. How do I survive and regain my balance in a foreign land where I feel disoriented and fragile? How do I keep my faith and my joy when I can't sense God and nothing feels familiar?

In my strong faith-filled moments I know this "land between" is fertile ground for God to display his mercies in disguise. In my head I know this is the place where God teaches me to trust him more intimately and transforms me to make me stronger and beautiful from the inside out. I also know how God wants to display his love and glory during desert wanderings. But knowing all this, how do I muster up enough faith in God to trust him to help me navigate this new and horrifying season in my life?

At that point in my spiritual journey, I was well acquainted with the story of Moses rescuing the Israelites from Egypt and living in the desert for 40 years. God used Moses to rescue the Israelites from the grip of Pharaoh after decades of slavery. Moses was to deliver his people to the promised land. God wanted to bring his beloved people to a land of abundance with all the opulence and provisions they would ever need. But why did they have to endure the hardships of those years in the desert?

Jeff Manion in his popular book *The Land Between* interprets it this way: "God allowed the Israelites to endure hardship in the desert so he could provide for them, so they would learn trust and dependence … Often God leads us through the land we most want to avoid in order to produce the fruit we most desperately desire."[33]

During their residency in Egypt, the Israelites were enmeshed with idols and pagan worship. God needed to withdraw them into the desert to get the strongholds of Egypt out of them and demolish their false beliefs. He wanted them to know that he was their God, their provider, protection, and provision. To visually demonstrate his faithful presence he appeared to them as a cloud during the day to give them shade and a pillar of fire at night to give them warmth. God was close to them 24-7 for all those years so that the people would know he was their El-Roi, the God who sees. God was their Yahweh Rapha, the Lord who heals, and Yahweh Shalom, the Lord who is peace. He was everything to them, and he wanted his people to trust him and allow him to guide them to their promised land.

We always have a choice. We get to decide whether we will learn to trust God with every aspect of our lives and embrace the promised land or allow bitterness, fear, or rebellion to foolishly guide our way. The Israelites did not get to enjoy their land flowing with milk and honey, because they didn't trust God and were afraid. What a sad and tragic story of opportunities lost. I did not want this to happen to me during my first desert experience, after the death of Dick, and then my second "land between," after Jack's death. I was determined to embrace my promised land and rediscover joy and fullness of life. Desperately seeking God's guidance, I chose to come out of my barren land wiser, stronger, more joyful, and with a deepened trust relationship with my Jehovah.

I consider myself a student of God's Word. I love the narratives, God's promises, words of hope, and eating his words that are as sweet as honey. I've discovered there's a time for studying God's Word and enjoying knowing his promises, and then comes a time of testing to see if the words took root. While I was in the "land between," there were a few ways I had to learn to trust God implicitly.

1. God Is Always Beside Us

With arms lifted up we raise our joyful voices to sing worship songs and declare we know that our Saviour lives and is always with us. There are endless verses in the Bible to remind us: "Never will I leave you; never will I forsake you" (Heb. 13:5). But when we're in the desert, with a dry and parched throat, desperately looking for water, we need to believe that God is with us. Even when we can't see that God is working or feel that he is

---

33. Jeff Manion, *The Land Between: Finding God in Difficult Transitions* (Grand Rapids: Zondervan, 2010), 54, 191.

making a new way, we have to know he is beside us, fulfilling his promises and bringing light into our darkness. We have to nurture a deeper knowing of God's character, to the depth where we know God's love so personally and intimately that even though our bodies are knocked over by the gale forces of desert winds, our souls remain strong and resilient. During the barren season of life we need to be reminded that he is with us even when it doesn't look or feel like it.

Mary stood outside the tomb crying, and as she wept, she stooped and looked in. Jesus—gone. Hope—lost. Two angels sat where Jesus's body had lain.

> They asked her, "Woman, why are you crying?"
>
> "They have taken my Lord away," she said, "and I don't know where they have put him." At this, she turned around and saw Jesus standing there, but she did not realize that it was Jesus.
>
> He asked her, "Woman, why are you crying? Who is it you are looking for?"
>
> Thinking he was the gardener, she said, "Sir, if you have carried him away, tell me where you have put him, and I will get him."
>
> Jesus said to her, "Mary." (John 20:13–16)

Then she turned and realized it was her Lord. He had been there the whole time, but she did not recognize him.

Our Christian faith becomes steadfast and real when we know without a doubt that God is at work even when we can't see anything happening or changing. It's so easy to say to someone, "Don't worry about it; God is with you. He's got this!" But we have to get to that place of trust where we have a settled assurance he is right beside us even when we don't recognize him.

Jacob and his mother, Rebekah, did the unthinkable. Together they deceived Jacob's twin brother, Esau, and stole Esau's blessing. After the manipulation and fateful debacle, when Esau came to receive his blessing and found out he'd been deceived by his brother, with a broken heart he cried out to his father. "'Oh my father, what about me? Bless me, too!' he begged" (Gen. 27:34 NLT). It was time for Jacob to hit the road because Esau was going to kill him. "Esau hated Jacob because their father had given Jacob the blessing. And Esau began to scheme: 'I will soon be mourning my father's death. Then I will kill my brother, Jacob'" (Gen. 27:41 NLT).

Jacob, fearing for his life, fled to Paddan-Aram, and at sundown he set up camp at a place called Bethel. Jacob found a stone to rest his head against and fell asleep. As he slept, he had a dream and saw a stairway going up to heaven, and he saw angels of God going up and down the staircase. The Lord stood at the top of the staircase and promised Jacob that the ground he was lying on would belong to him and his descendants. When Jacob awoke from his sleep he said, "Surely the LORD is in this place, and I wasn't even aware of it!" (Gen. 28:16 NLT).

These two stories had a profound impact on how I perceived God while in the "land between." Even when it didn't feel like anything was changing or happening, I had a deep *knowing* that he was with me.

2. Everything in Life Is Temporary

I know it hurt my children to watch me suffering with intense grief and PTSD. My stepdaughter, Janice, is a lovely, wise, and kind woman. She's a doctor, wife, mother of three boys, and avid biker and hiker. The fall of 2019 she spent a month in Nepal and hiked up to 17,000 feet on the Manaslu Circuit, which goes around Manaslu Himal, the eighth highest mountain in the world. Not only is she a great athlete; she's also very insightful. One day during my intense grief while we were visiting online, she gave voice to one sentence that changed my landscape. She said, "Mom, everything in life is temporary." I knew this, but her verbalizing it cemented it and shaped it into a more concrete understanding. *Of course,* I thought, *the seasons come and go. After the harsh cold winter the ground breaks open to make room for the daffodils. Trees burn down and grow back. We cut our finger, and it heals. After the indigo night every sunrise is a spectacular gift from God, and after the rain God paints the rainbows to remind us of his unfailing promises.* Psalm 23 reminded me that "Even though I walk **through** the darkest valley, I will fear no evil, for you are with me" (Ps. 23:4, emphasis added). Not only do I walk **through** my "land between"; I'm also never alone. Then I was reminded, "Because of the LORD's great love we are not consumed, for his compassions never fail. They are new every morning; great is your faithfulness" (Lam. 3:22–23). Wow, what a promise!

This simple but heartfelt revelation was a refreshing oasis to my short-sighted view of my desert. It changed the perspective of my murky future to know that joy was still there—it just needed time to break through the dry and parched terrain.

3. Power Starts on Our Knees

God's purpose for the Israelites' wandering in the desert was to teach them to obey God's commandments and learn to trust him for their provisions and protection. It wasn't long before the Israelites started whining and complaining about everything. At one point they wanted meat, and Moses had no idea how he was going to provide meat for all those people. The Lord heard their grumbling and responded with "Is the LORD's arm too short? Now you will see whether or not what I say will come true for you" (Num. 11:23). In other words, "Moses, are you questioning my ability, my power to provide?"

God is our Jehovah-Jireh: the Lord will provide. He wants us to come to him on our knees with humble and honest heartfelt prayers. Trust is the glue that holds relationships together, and trust starts on our knees. He wants us to look to him for answers and guidance because he is the only one who can do the impossible. This promise is available to us through Jesus's own words: "With man this is impossible, but not with God; all things are possible with God" (Mark 10:27). If you look to God to do the impossible, a good place to start is on your knees, asking him some questions:

- "God, how did I get here, and how do I move forward?"
- "God, what do you want me to do?" "Is there someone I need to forgive?"
- "God, how did I get into this rut?" "How do I find my new purpose?"
- "God, why is this happening?" "Is there something I should be aware of?"

During my desert wandering when the enemy's lies and deceit taunted me to believe I was knocked down and would never again get up, I got down on my knees. It was the sweetest place on earth. That's where I found my answers, my peace, and the courage to move forward and onward. By bringing me to my knees, God taught me to trust him in my desert place.

4. God Wants Us to Ask for Help

Pride and self-sufficiency build a rebellious barrier that may sabotage God's power to move us out of the desert.

Like many of you, I'm an "I'll do it myself" woman. I recall during the harsh and endless winter after Jack's death standing in my front entryway, tears streaming down my face, wearing my old slippers and ugly red housecoat, asking a total stranger, "Will you please shovel my driveway this winter?" I have a long, winding driveway, and Jack had always tended to the shovelling. Being all alone, I couldn't do it. I was too sick. I needed help. I had to ask.

I needed other people to help me, and I became good at asking for many things. In fact, if we don't ask, we deprive many people of being used by God to pour out a blessing. People around us are God's hands and feet. We need our heart-connection friends, counsellors, mentors, and doctors.

5. We Declare Joy in a Stance of Victory

To get us out of the desert and into our promised land we have to foster the positive and forward thinking attitude of Caleb. He was one of the ten spies who went into Canaan, and he gave this report to Moses: "We should go up and take possession of the land, for we can certainly do it" (Num. 13:30). While negativity and fear infested the camp, Caleb declared victory. I love this!

God is not going to give us all the details or a blueprint for how our life is going to unfold. If we had all the facts, we would not need faith or learn to trust God. I love what Joel Osteen says about knowing details in his book *Blessed in the Darkness*:

There is a reason we don't have all the details. If we did, we wouldn't move into the fullness of our destiny because no one likes adversity. We love to be comfortable. But you won't become all you were created to be without opposition, challenges and difficulties that stretch and grow and use your spiritual muscles.[34]

In order to reclaim our joy and enter into our promised land, we must position ourselves in a stance of victory. Believing, we will not settle for mediocrity but go for the greatness God has placed in us. We may give up, but God never gives up on us. We cannot adopt a victim's mentality, because it becomes a victim's reality. But here's the good news: a victor's mentality becomes a victor's reality.

What a marvellous thing it is when we have been in the "land between," fallen apart, survived—and by the grace of God become more beautiful and joyful from the inside out.

GROW YOUR JOY

1. Upgrade your joy. We love upgrades. How exciting to have the latest model of our phone, a state of the art renovated kitchen, or a newer and flashier car. When something gets old or breaks down, we love a newer and better version. How about when you're a new widow, you break your ankle and are completely disabled for three months? That's what happened to my friend Carol Rath. In the midst of grieving the loss of her beloved Helmut, trying to sell her house, and maintaining a huge yard, Carol fell and broke her ankle. It was a severe break that needed surgery, and she was helpless for almost three months. When I visited with her, she wasn't grumbling or feeling sorry for herself; she was positive and victorious. With her face lit up with joy she couldn't wait to tell me,

> Heidi, you can't believe what joy I'm experiencing. I've never spent so much time in God's Word, and I'm learning truths I've never known before. After all these years of knowing God his love feels deeper and stronger. What a precious time I've had sitting here day after day learning more about love, forgiveness, and grace. It's been such a gift.

The only one who can stop your joy is you. My friend Carol decided she was going to upgrade her joy in spite of her temporary "land between."

2. Develop a "Godittude." Some of you reading this book know that your "land between" will end in heaven sooner than you had imagined. For over seven years my dearest friend of 44 years, Angie Selles, was in her "land between" called A.L.S. (Amyotrophic Lateral Sclerosis, also known as Lou Gehrig's disease), a disease that gradually paralyzes people because the brain is no longer able to communicate with the muscles of the body. While she was still able to speak, she told me she was developing her "Godittude." She explained it to me this way: "Heidi, I want my attitude to reflect

---

34. Joel Osteen, *Blessed In the Darkness: How All Things Are Working for Your Good* (New York: FaithWords, 2017), 180.

God's love and the joy he's put into my life." After Angie went into her eternal promised land on August 27, 2019, I was incredibly honoured to speak at her funeral and tell everyone about her determined "Godittude" choices, even when she could no longer form words. Her eyes and smile expressed the fruit of God's Spirit shining through her.

If Angie could develop this beautiful attitude while knowing her promised land was in heaven, imagine what we can do while going *through* our momentary affliction. Even when words fail us, we can chose to develop a "Godittude" in spite of the droughts and temporarily parched land. It's a daily choice to display an outer declaration of the joy that is within us. We can do this because we have assurance of endless joy in our final home: heaven.

3. Know that God is your rescuer. Hardships are meant to build trust, not contemptuous complaints. Jeff Manion talks about discipline in his book *The Land Between*. He says, "I have to wonder, when God disciplines us in ways that seem harsh or difficult to bear, could it be that he is attempting to rescue something?"[35] From the beginning of time God's work has always been to rescue his people.

The consequences of the Israelites rejecting the promised land caused them to wander in the desert for 40 years until that entire generation died. Why not save yourself all that pain and wandering around the same mountain and turn to God like Moses did? Moses had honest questions and worked with God. The Israelites grumbled and complained, and because of their fear and failure to trust God, that generation never stepped foot into their promised land. What a sad story of a failure to launch. What missed opportunities of not seeing God's abundant provisions!

Don't waste your pain. To recapture your joy, allow yourself to see the dark seasons as a place to build your trust in God. The God who brought the Israelites out of Egypt is also your rescuer and alongside you in the "land between." In order to become extraordinary, you have to encounter extraordinary trouble. And while you're rootless, God is building greatness.

---

35. Manion, *The Land Between*, 125.

AND ASK GOD TO MAKE YOU JOYFUL

Ask God, What do you want me to learn in the "land between"?

S—Scripture: "With man this is impossible, but not with God; all things are possible with God" (Mark 10:27).

T—Thanksgiving: Thank you, God; this verse brings life into my soul. Thank you that I can trust you with my life. Help me to remember this remarkable promise while I face days where I'm weary and wandering in a dry and parched land. Thank you that you never leave me or forsake me and are always rescuing me and showing me how to live with joy.

O—Observation: This verse reminds me that if God can create heaven and earth, he can do anything. Why do I forget God's power when I'm in the middle of trouble and heartbreak? I need to remember that God, who created me, knows me inside and out, knows my affliction, and is the only one who can rescue and transform me. He is the source of all goodness and the provider of my joy.

P—Prayer: Heavenly Father, in this moment, with open hands, I give you my anxiety, worry, and fear. Thank you that I am in the presence of the miraculous and that nothing is impossible for you. I'm hurting, and I ask that you join me in my place of discomfort. I need your strength, your mercy, and your comfort. Show me ways I can trust you, and let me know my part in coming out of the "land between." Help me not to be the victim but to embrace this journey in a stance of victory. Help me to know you are with me, and show me ways I can learn to trust you more. Use this time to draw me closer to you and fill me anew with fresh joy. Thank you. Amen.

MOVING FORWARD TO JOY
GETTING UNSTUCK

"No one can get Joy by merely asking for it. It is one of the ripest
fruits of the Christian life, and, like all fruits, must be grown."
—Henry Drummond (1884)

I was stuck. No going forward or backward, and the harder I tried to get out of the snowbank, the deeper I went. It was March 2019, and for ten days I was Nana for three of my glorious grandchildren in Grassy Lake, Alberta. In the second week of my visit, a freak snowstorm bombarded Southern Alberta and embedded our house and highways in snowbanks. I'm their Nana, and snowstorms were not going to stop me from driving my grandchildren to skating, volleyball, and birthday parties. I'd lived in Alberta from 1981 to 1993, so I was familiar with blizzards, whiteouts, and unexpected snowdrifts. Also, I had my son-in-law's great SUV with winter tires, and I was a confident all-seasons driver. But it all fell apart when it was time to take my granddaughter Mya to her friend's birthday party.

Pulling into the driveway of Mya's friend's home, I swerved and spun the strong Acadia through the deep snow and dodged the snowbanks. Success. Phew, I made it to the front entryway. Then I turned the vehicle around, smiled, and waved goodbye to the partygoers hovering at the living room window. Then I navigated my wheels smack dab into a snowbank and was stuck.

Stepping on the gas only dug me in deeper. I was going nowhere. The partygoers at the window were waving and laughing at the city girl who didn't know how to drive in the snow. It was humiliating, and I needed help.

I am so grateful for friendly Alberta farmers with their huge farm machinery and big neighbourly hearts. Ryan, the father of the birthday girl, saw my dilemma and cheerfully asked the rhetorical question: "Hey, neighbour, do you need some help?" My humble "Yes, please" didn't explain everything else going on in my mind. *Ryan, if you weren't here today I would really be pooched. I have no idea how I would get this monster vehicle out of this mess. Sometimes I feel so alone, but then God brings me just what I need. I am so grateful for people who take the time to care.*

Within minutes a huge tractor circled the field and pulled up to the SUV, and Ryan pulled out a long industrial-looking chain. He shimmied under the vehicle to affix the chain to the bumper, attached the other end to the tractor, and told me to get into the Acadia and put it into neutral. The big tractor went to work, and inch by inch I was dislodged from the nasty snowdrift. I was lightheaded with relief and threw my arms around Ryan's neck to thank him for coming alongside me and getting me unstuck. Again I saw how we always need something bigger than ourselves to get us moving forward.

GETTING UNSTUCK

We feel horrible and helpless when we're stuck. We can't go back, and we've no idea how to move forward. We feel depleted, and for sure the joy has gone. It's one thing for someone to have a huge piece of machinery to help winch us out of a snowbank, but it's another story when we're stuck in hopelessness, despair, or an adversity without hope for finding resolve. There are times in life when our thoughts tell us, *You've seen your last good days. The layoff was your fault, and now you've lost your career. You're unlovable; that's why he left you. This illness is the end of you. You'll never dig yourself out of this financial mess.*

During my season of PTSD and grief, God gave me a clear picture of how to move forward. The concept is so simple that it took me by surprise. It's hard to imagine a majestic God, who created the universe, using simplistic tools to help us tap into abundant joy. But he knows how to get our attention. There is a commanding verse in the Bible that tells us how to get what we need: "Do not be deceived: God cannot be mocked. A man reaps what he sows" (Gal. 6:7). How can that short and puzzling verse help us to get unstuck?

GIFT OF SEEDS

Everything starts with a seed. "Your thoughts are seed. Your words are seed. Whatever becomes of your life, what becomes of you, is first sowed in your mind and in your heart."[36] Sowing of seeds is not meant to frighten or intimidate us, but it's part of God's divine plan to help us live a fruitful, abundant, and joyful life. It's really so simple.

---

36. Phillip Chidavaenzi, "The Spiritual Law of Sowing and Reaping," *The Standard* (May 29, 2018).

I see this every year at my daughter Michelle's family's farmland. Each spring, her husband, Tim, and his band of workers sow approximately 35 to 40 different seeds. I love it when my grandson Austin takes me around to their seed bins and explains, "Nana, these are chickpeas, this is barley, over here is oats, and these are lentils." Austin knows his seeds, and from the time he was three he knew that when his dad sows barley, he's not going to get oats. When his dad sows wheat, he won't get corn, and lentil seeds don't produce peas. Good seeds produce good food. But here's the bad news: Bad seeds produce bad food.

- When we sow jealousy, how can we have love and joy in relationships?
- When we plant unforgiveness, how can we expect a loving and harmonious relationship with God and each other?
- When we plant hatred and anger, how can we expect to have good marriages and raise godly children?
- If we plant revenge, how will we experience peace?
- When we plant criticism and judgment, how can we expect to be embraced and loved?
- If we plant betrayal, how can we expect that we will never be betrayed?

Every time we open our mouth, we're planting a seed. The Bible makes it clear: "Words kill, words give life; they're either poison or fruit—you choose" (Prov. 18:21 MSG). God is a good, good father who wants to pour good things into our lives, and if we want to live our very best life, we must be willing to plant good seeds. In spite of what we're going through, we can all sow good seeds. If you want something, you have to sow seeds to get it.

SEEDS GROW IN THE DARKNESS

At one time or another all of us go through a dark place, divorce, sickness, bankruptcy, or heartbreak from a child. God uses the dark, silent, and lonely places to plant seeds of joy and greatness. Joel Osteen's perspective on the topic of seeds is so refreshing:

> As long as a seed remains in the light, it cannot germinate and will never become what it was created to be. The seed must be planted in the soil, in a dark place, so that the potential on the inside will come to life. In the same way, there are seeds of greatness in us—dreams, goals, talents, potential—that will only come to life in a dark place.[37]

It's hard to comprehend that while I was in the darkness of grief and pain, my soul was fertile ground for greatness and fresh joy. The year after Jack's death was the darkest

---

37. Osteen, *Blessed In the Darkness*, 16.

night of my soul, and I desperately wanted hope and my joy back. In spite of my wobbly legs and my mind acting like a sieve, I intentionally started to plant seeds.

First, I wanted hope, and here is how I started:

- With the help of the Bible Gateway app, I looked up all the verses on hope and devoured the sweetness of them. I felt like the prophet Ezekiel, who said, "When I ate it, it tasted as sweet as honey in my mouth" (Ezek. 3:3 NLT).
- I asked friends to help me find the best books written on hope. I consumed my favourite book *The Hope Habit: Finding God's Goodness When Life Is Hard*, by Terry Law and Jim Gilbert. It awakened my soul to find hope beyond my present prison and foggy future.
- In spite of my pain, I reached out to other people who were going through dark times. By planting hope in their lives, I was preparing hope for me.
- I fervently and diligently prayed for hope. I begged the Holy Spirit to fill me with living water to germinate the seeds and spring forth hope.
- I blogged and wrote articles on hope.

By doing this I was planting seeds, and they were starting to germinate. Two things happened:

1. Hope became a reality. God's promises were trustworthy, and I started to feel alive. This next verse was a lifeline: "May the God of hope fill you with all joy and peace as you trust in him, so that you may overflow with hope by the power of the Holy Spirit" (Rom. 15:13). The book *The Hope Habit* sums it up perfectly: "True hope, then, is certain of God's goodness and sees reality in light of it."[38] Yes, once again I was assured of God's promises for a good future. Finding hope was the first step to recapturing my joy.
2. It spurred me on to plant more seeds. This time I was ready for joy.

By now I knew the power of sowing and reaping, and I began to sow seeds of joy. I posted about joy on all facets of social media. I read books on joy and studied the Bible and ate words of joy. I found ways to bless other people and gave gifts. I took friends to lunch, invited joyful conversations, and instigated laughter. My soul began to see light, and I started to prosper. The Bible promises this: "Be kind and good to others; then you will live safely here in the land and prosper" (Ps. 37:3 TLB). It's the concept of sowing and reaping. If you do this, then this will happen:

---

38. Terry Law and Jim Gilbert, *The Hope Habit: Finding God's Goodness When Life is Hard* (Lake Mary: Charisma House, 2010), 27.

- If you want friends, sow seeds of friendship.
- If you are lonely and discouraged, don't sit around and feel sorry for yourself. Go find somebody, and cheer him or her up.
- If you want joy, go and sow some joy.
- If you want a happy marriage, sow kindness, forgiveness, and grace.
- If you want to be understood, be someone who seeks to understand.

Everything we sow will come back to us at just the right time. You and I have powerful influence wherever we go, in our homes, churches, places of recreation, and community. We can bring words of destruction or strife or words of life and be world changers. That power is in our words and under our control.

SEEDS OF KINDNESS

I have a sign in my home that says, "Kindness is beautiful." If I have to choose a favourite seed, I pick the seed of kindness. The Bible tells us to "love one another," and I've come to realize that kindness is the most powerful expression of love in action. The Bible tells us that it's to be our highest aim: "whatever you do, do it with kindness and love" (1 Cor. 16:14 TLB). Wow, whatever we do—that's a high and noble calling. But think back to how you feel when someone says,

- "You look tired and overwhelmed; how can I help you?"
- "I know you're not feeling well; I'll bring supper tonight."
- "Let me give you a break and take your children for the afternoon."
- "Here is some money to get you through the next couple of weeks."
- "Can I give you a ride to the airport?"

After reading close to a thousand sympathy cards and reflecting on comments about Jack, I can summarize all those words into one sentence: "Jack was the kindest man I've ever met." For those people who knew Jack and are reading this book, I am sure you will agree with those words. Jack was the incarnation of kindness and was loved by people wherever he went because of this greatest expression and actions of love.

After Jack's funeral our family held hands, stood in a circle, and acknowledged we wanted to continue the legacy of kindness. With a large family of children and grandchildren of all ages, every once in a while we have to remind ourselves to accept and allow certain things because we've declared that "We're a family of kindness." Kindness is the highest expression of love because it is rooted in grace. Not only is it the greatest gift we can give away, but it's also the pathway to salvation and a personal relationship with our heavenly Father.

That's what happened to Rahab, the prostitute in chapter 2 and 3 in the book of Joshua. The people of Israel were finally crossing the Jordan River to inhabit the long-awaited promised land. But first they had to destroy the city of Jericho. Joshua, as a final preparation, sent out two spies to investigate the military strength of Jericho.

Rahab was an unlikely character to help the Israelites destroy that formidable city. She was a pagan, a Canaanite, and a prostitute, and yet she was the perfect pick. With the people coming and going in her home at all hours of the day and night, she would be the centre of the latest gossip and news. Rahab was willing to risk everything to protect the two spies because her heart had melted with fear when she heard of the Israelites' extraordinary powerful God. The God who parted the Red Sea, defeated Sihon and Og, the two kings of the Amorites, and defeated the mighty and wicked armies across the Jordan River. Out of fear and reverence for this miracle-making God, she hid the two spies under the flax on her rooftop, and because of her kindness she beseeched them, "Now then, please swear to me by the LORD that you will show kindness to my family, because I have shown kindness to you" (Josh. 2:12).

Rahab sowed seeds of kindness, saved the lives of the spies and her whole family, and ultimately helped to destroy the city of Jericho. Joshua 6:25 says that days after the city was destroyed, "Joshua spared Rahab the prostitute, with her family and all who belonged to her, because she hid the men Joshua had sent as spies to Jericho—and she lives among the Israelites to this day." Her reaping happened within days, but the supreme declaration of this seed reached its fruition some 1,420 years later with the birth of Jesus Christ. Rahab is recorded in the genealogy of Jesus Christ.

You might say, "Well, Heidi, those are great stories for you and Rahab, but I've been sowing good seeds for years, and I've not experienced any reaping." We have to remember that the reaping always comes at just the right time: when we need it. Some seeds sprout and flourish right away, and others take time. For all the years that Jack and I both sowed kindness, I was blessed to reap it exactly when I needed it.

- My stepson David helped me with all my financial stuff at a time when I needed it.
- The first winter, I was too sick to shovel the snow in my long driveway. God sent just the right people at the right time.
- I never needed help with repairs around the house before Jack's death. Now God gave me people to help with all the frustrating and bewildering things that were breaking and needed fixing.

When we sow seeds of kindness we sow the heart of God.

WE'RE NEVER STUCK

We're never stuck—don't let Satan lie to you. The Bible warns us, "Stay alert! Watch out for your great enemy the devil. He prowls around like a roaring lion, looking for someone to devour" (1 Pet. 5:8 NLT). You may have been sowing negative seeds without realizing it. The enemy uses the negativity and lies to pull us deeper into self-sabotage and defeat. What words are you sowing? Can you identify with any of these?

- Nothing good will ever come of this. I'm stuck.
- Nothing I do is ever good enough.
- I hate my job. I hate my life.
- I'll never get out of this mess.
- I'm unlovable.

If you have a good need, grow a good seed. In Mark Batterson's book *If*, he lays it out succinctly: "The next time you have a need, try sowing a seed at your point of need. Then watch the way God supplies all our needs, according to His riches in glory."[39] If you want something, sow a seed to get it.

- Do you want to be blessed? Sow blessings.
- Do you want freedom? Sow forgiveness.
- Do you want purpose? Go and serve.
- Do you want people to accept and love you? Sow kindness.

When you sow good seeds, you will reap goodness at just the right time. The seeds you sow now will reap themselves in your marriage, your children, your grandchildren, and beyond into the next generations. Are you stuck? Do you want your life to be transformed? Go sow some good seeds and experience fresh joy.

GROW YOUR JOY

1. Don't waste your pain. The stinky stuff in our lives—betrayal, rejection, and failure—is the fertilizer that prepares your seed to grow. In the same way that fertilizer causes your flowers and plants to explode with beauty and colour, God can take your past pain and mess and use them for your greater purpose, pleasure, and joy. It's in the dark places that you grow and your character is developed. When I speak at a conference I often tell my audiences, "Don't waste your pain. Let God make something purposeful and meaningful out of it." Seeds germinate in the dark but grow and flourish in the light. Once we decide to let God's light, the power of the Holy Spirit, illuminate our messes, God will transform our life in ways we could never have imagined.

---

39. Batterson, *If*, 154.

2. Flourish in the light. The parable of the sower in Mark 4:14–20 is a magnificent story of what happens when God's seed produces a bountiful harvest. The end of the parable goes like this: "Others, like seed sown on good soil, hear the word, accept it, and produce a crop—some thirty, some sixty, some a hundred times what was sown" (Mark 4:20).

My friend and mentor Margaret Gibb, the founder and director of Women Together, is a great example of someone who was stuck but then truly accepted God's message to sow seeds around the world. She listened and was obedient to the prompting of the Holy Spirit with the words (seeds) God put in her heart. But Margaret is wise and knows she can't do it alone. She partnered with the light and power of the Holy Spirit to produce and multiply an unimaginable harvest. Seeds flourish in the light of the Holy Spirit, and as Margaret always says, "God can do *more* than we can ever imagine."

Since 2007 Margaret has been to 19 countries and made 37 overseas trips. These countries include Uganda, Tanzania, Kenya, Ukraine, Thailand, England, Germany, India, Philippines, Israel, Brazil, Argentina, France, Italy, Russia, Siberia, Colombia, Armenia, and the United States. Women Together has provided 14 alumni scholarships and currently has 6 students in Siberia, India, Nepal, Uganda, Kenya, and Brazil. She created and developed an online magazine that is published in Russian and reaches 24 countries. Since 2018 she partnered with other Canadian authors to publish not just one but two books. And there is much more. But it would take pages to list the reaping from the magnificent seeds that have grown and flourished. When Margaret took God's Word, planted it in fertile ground, and let the Holy Spirit water it with God's power, not only was she unstuck; she experienced joy beyond anything she could have imagined.[40]

It's never easy, but when you and I are obedient to the message God places in our hearts, it produces a harvest of 30, 60, or 100 times as much as was planted in our hearts.

3. Use the dark times to pray more. Our most powerful prayer times probably don't take place in a chaise lounge beside the pool at the Holiday Inn. It's in the dark and lonely places that we break through our self-sufficiency and pray fervently. Prayer is where character seeds are developed. Be intentional about using the dark and devastating times in your life to pray for the seeds that will not only get you unstuck but produce a bountiful and unfathomable harvest. We are assured that God hears our prayers and will produce the kind of harvest that is unleashing our very best life. The Bible tells us, "The earnest prayer of a righteous person has great power and produces wonderful results" (James 5:16 NLT). Prayer is the fertilizer that grows our seeds. While we wait for results prayer not only changes our hearts; it sprouts tendrils of new joy. When we grow closer to God in prayer, we grow in joy.

---

40. Used with permission from Margaret Gibb.

4. Awaken your senses. Joy is rooted in the truth of who God is and that he has a purposeful plan for your life. Even when we don't see or feel anything happening, God is always at work in the background. So while you're waiting for results, go out and stir up some joy seeds.

Joy embraces all our senses, and we become fully awake with the sights, sounds, and smells that delight us. While I was in my waiting period I awakened my senses by surrounding myself with beauty. For me beauty is expressed through listening to water sounds, burning aromatic candles, and treating myself to fresh flowers and colourful decor. I expanded my senses by repainting some walls and hanging pictures that evoked a smile. I placed soft and colourful pillows on my couches and surrounded myself with books that kindled curiosity and stimulated my soul. Then I turned on my favourite music app and sang out loud! Surrounding myself with colours and sounds that delighted me reduced my stress, helped me sleep better, and produced feelings of well-being.

5. Don't forget to count your blessings. Counting our blessings is not a one-time event; it's an ongoing process that helps us to move forward. Remembering God's goodness brings fresh perspective and reminds us that there is beauty all around. Writing in my thankful journal helped me to get unstuck, move forward, and plant seeds of hope and joy.

2974. People who reach out
2991. Friends texting encouragement
3006. My shovelling angels
3021. Bright sunshine today
3048. Feeling a bit stronger today
3055. Reading on the couch by the fire
3016. Being hugged

Yes, a tractor and heavy chain will get us out of a snowbank. A year-end bonus will temporarily solve the monthly financial crisis. A new car will help us get to work every day. But spiritually and emotionally, the only place we're stuck is in our mind. Sowing good seeds will help us to move forward with purpose and joy and produce a great harvest.

Think of one apple seed. Imagine how one seed can produce another tree with perhaps 300 more apples. All things being equal, one apple tree produces about 1,500 seeds per season. Those 1,500 seeds potentially produce 450,000 apples and 2,250,000 seeds. This process goes on and on. Imagine what you can reap when you sow seeds of joy. If you want something, sow some seeds. Go and grow some joy.

AND ASK GOD TO MAKE YOU JOYFUL

Ask God, What seeds do I need to plant?

S—Scripture: "Be kind and good to others; then you will live safely here in the land and prosper" (Ps. 37:3 TLB).

T—Thanksgiving: Thank you, God, that you are the kindest person I have ever met. Thank you that you have placed the Spirit of kindness in me and that it is available to me at all times. Kindness is one of the greatest gifts you can give me, and I thank you for it.

O—Observation: The spiritual verse about sowing and reaping is hard to comprehend. I always thought that to have joy I needed more of something—more money, accomplishments, stuff, and loving relationships. Sowing seems too simple and yet too hard. To think that if I want joy I have to go out and plant seeds of kindness and goodness—it's a mind-blowing concept.

P—Prayer: God, teach me the practice of sowing and reaping. Show me how I can plant kindness and goodness so that I prosper in spirit. God, I want to have faith as tiny as a mustard seed so I can watch it grow into a fruit-bearing tree, a tree that will not only prosper but also bring shade for when I'm weary. Help me to keep my eyes on you so that I can watch you do what I think is impossible. Thank you that nothing is too hard for you and I can come to you with all my needs. Help me to sow seeds of kindness. Thank you. Amen.

JOY WHEN WE KNOW WHO WE ARE
A LESSON FROM MY PUTTER

"Joy is the divine reward for discerning the divine purpose of the immediate moment." —Attributed to Mike Murdock

What an annoyance. It was a perfect summer day, and I was getting ready to golf on one of my favourite courses with my best friends, but there was no putter in my golf bag. Sighing with frustration and disappointment, I knew I had either lost my putter or left it at home. I wasn't going to let this little hiccup stop my golf game. Confidently I walked into the pro shop and asked if they had any old putters lying around, one I could use for the eighteen-hole game.

Moments later the attendant brought out an old Ping putter and shrugged, saying, "This ancient one's been around for a long time and no one is using it, so here you go." It was not a piece of equipment I would have picked, but I was grateful and thanked the attendant profusely.

A few holes into the game, that old worn-out stick gave me some good putts. I loved the weight and the way it handled, and I decided I liked it. When it was time to hand the putter back to the pro shop, I asked the same attendant if I could buy it. Again with an indifferent tone, he mumbled, "Well, it's been there for a long time, and we don't know who it belongs to, so I'll sell it to you for twenty-five dollars." Done. Sold.

I now had a new old putter. In fact, it was so old and cheap I didn't take care of it. Several times I almost lost it by leaving it beside a putting green. For the next few months it served me well, so I decided to take it into my favourite golf shop to freshen it up with a new grip. My friend Doug was behind the counter when I picked up my regripped putter, and he had a mischievous grin on his face.

"Heidi, where did you get this putter, and do you know anything about it?" he asked. I relayed the story of how I acquired the putter, and then his next words blew me away. "Do you know," Doug said, "this is an antique and worth a lot of money?" Doug pulled out a book and showed me a picture of my putter and the present market value. I was speechless. I had a treasure, a masterpiece, and all this time I didn't even know it. I turned down Doug's offer to buy it and tucked this precious piece of equipment under my arm and went home.

Since I acquired the putter in 2003, several people have begged to buy it. I've always said "no" because now I truly value my putter. Knowing its value I now treat it differently. I've given it a protective head cover and another new grip, and I always know where it is. After I finish at each putting green, I wipe the putter clean and carefully put it back into my bag. I treat my putter with respect and good care because it has great value and it gives me joy.

JOY WHEN WE KNOW WHO WE ARE

Wouldn't it be wonderful if we could take the humdrum out of our day and stop at a store or a drive-through on the way to work and buy a daily cup of joy? There are endless frustrations and struggles in this world, so how about a gallon of joy that will last all day?

I know that Jesus desires us to have fullness of joy. He spent three years with his disciples teaching them how to obey his commandments and remain in his love so they could have this daily dose of joy. Here is how he summed it up: "I have told you this so that my joy may be in you and that your joy may be complete" (John 15:11). Wouldn't we all love joy that is finished, faultless, and superb? It's hard to imagine this in the present society where our happiness is achieved through success in careers, accomplishments, adventures, and stuff. So how can we tap into the overflowing and unlimited joy that is available to us through Jesus's teaching? It starts by knowing who we are and respecting our God-given value.

Throughout the two years following Jack's death, I would have despaired had I not spent the previous 30 years knowing my value in Christ and learning to respect and protect my heart. After the death of my first husband, Dick, my self-esteem and value were shaken to the core. For years I didn't know who I was. So much of me was imbedded in my children's accomplishments, the success of my husband's career, and my pride in running a law firm. In order to survive and become a joyful and confident woman, I knew I had to discern who and what would define me and where I would find my value. Would it be the world or who I was in Christ? I continue to dig into God's promises and daily declare to live by them. I have four guiding principles that help me find my value in Christ:

- **Reject self-condemnation**. "Therefore, there is now no condemnation for those who are in Christ Jesus" (Rom. 8:1). This means stopping self-judgment and forgiving ourselves for our past sins. But the hardest part is letting go of the shame that accompanies our powerlessness to accept our flaws, weaknesses, and inability to be perfect. God forgives our sins, but our shame needs to be surrendered. Once I learned the concept of surrendering my shame and leaving it at the cross, my spirit had a revolutionary shift, and for the first time in my life I felt free to be who God made me to be. Daily I absolutely refuse to allow false guilt or shame to render me hopeless or helpless.

- **Accept God's lavish love.** "See what great love the Father has lavished on us, that we should be called children of God!" (1 John 3:1). Years ago, when I looked in the mirror I saw only my flaws and inabilities. It took years of studying God's promises and asking him over and over again to help me receive and feel his love in a tangible way. Over time God's lavish love has become the unshakable and unstoppable truth that is now the anchor of my soul and has sustained me through many storms. Knowing my heavenly Father lavishly loves me propels me to be a warrior for the truth of who I am in Christ.

- **Extend grace to others and myself**. I used to love perfection, rules, and deadlines and used them to impose their rules on others and myself. But instead of these high standards and obligations producing fulfillment and joy, they produced self-righteousness and pride. By battling through the journey of applying truth to my heart, ultimately I grasped the immeasurable concept of the grace Christ poured out for me on the cross. But it can't stop there; I must extend this grace to everyone in all aspects of my duties and relationships. What freedom! What joy to let go of petty irritations and unrealistic expectations! I'm sure most people in my life were relieved when I began to understand the verse "My grace is sufficient for you, for my power is made perfect in weakness" (2 Cor. 12:9).

- **Declare that I have a joyful purpose**. It took me years to understand and accept this last and most important principle: I am God's masterpiece, and he has good things for me to do. God has a glorious purpose for my life, and I love the way Katie Brazelton describes this in her book *Pathway to Purpose.* She says, the joy of glorifying God by doing his work can be so powerful that you may wonder if it's wrong—as in sinful wrong—to feel so extremely satisfied while doing it. This may be particularly true if you feel you don't deserve to be happy, if you were raised to believe that reality is always tough, or if you have thought that ministry is supposed to be a tedious obligation. But believe me, it is not a sin to feel God's pleasure as you fulfill his plans for your life. It is his gift.[41]

I want to jump for joy and cheer as Katie continues on, "This magnificent idea of allowing us to feel joy—to feel fulfilled and satisfied while doing the Lord's work—is to me one of God's most awesome gifts."[42]

Having the privilege of doing the Lord's work joyfully means we get up each morning, fill our cup with coffee, and set our feet in motion for a divine purpose. But we know there are unexpected and sometimes ugly interruptions when we lose our equilibrium and gasp for air.

My dear friend Candace Giesbrecht experienced a startling discovery after the birth of their long-awaited son Cohen. Here is her story of finding her value and purpose. It started with just needing to get out of the house and get perspective.

"Just walk to the end of the street and back. I'll watch the baby." My husband's eyes were pleading, gentle, pained, and firm. I argued with him, saying I understood his kind intent, but a walk to the end of road wasn't going to change anything. Tears wet my cheeks as I walked out of the house wishing I could remember what to do with my hands. There seemed to be no point. I was tired and felt so lost.

My body was created to mother this new baby boy, and while I was overwhelmed and relieved at how wildly I loved him, I was certain I was doing everything wrong. The evidence was stacking up everywhere I turned. Suggestions that I had overdressed or underdressed my baby came from well-meaning women in waiting rooms. Comments about when I should have responded more or less quickly to his cries were offered without permission. One mom actually laughed when she saw me awkwardly trying to navigate all my stuff and then pronounced, "You are sooo out of your element."

I knew my identity was wrapped up in my work and in achievements and adjusting to motherhood would be tougher for me than perhaps for others. What I didn't know was that many women who experience depression after the birth of their babies actually begin to experience symptoms during pregnancy.

---

41. Katie Brazelton, *Pathway to Purpose for Women* (Grand Rapids: Zondervan, 2005), 223.
42. Brazelton, *Pathway to Purpose for Women*, 223.

Looking back, I think symptoms started for me in my second trimester. All I knew was that this was supposed to be the happiest and most fulfilled time in my life and yet my mood was lower than ever.

I had so much to be grateful for, but somehow focusing on this only made me feel guilty. I needed a spiritual reboot! I was afraid of what I would lose if I rebooted and just kept running with a slow, outdated and inadequate operating system. Through the love, care and diligent prayer of a few key women in my life, including a mentor-coach, I began reordering my thoughts, my behaviours and my heart. Scripture and intentional surrender brought me first to my knees and then slowly back to standing on my feet. Only this time, I was standing on the solid rock of Christ rather than the shifting sands of accomplishments, responsibilities, and external validations.

As my heart shifted, so did my face. Friends who hadn't seen me in months asked me what secret I was keeping. I recall a total stranger asking me why my eyes were so bright. I had learned to surrender. I had learned to practice taking my everyday, ordinary life—my sleeping, eating, going to work, and walking around life—and place it before God as an offering (see Rom. 12:1). As my faith, value and purpose deepened, true joy rang in my heart.[43]

Candace gives a candid glimpse into the lives of many other women like her. May we learn from each other to find our value and purpose in who Christ made us to be. All of us are different and unique, and God has a fulfilling purpose of each one of us.

JOY WHEN WE KNOW WHOSE WE ARE

Joy is linked to Jesus. The apostle Paul clearly knew who he was. In most of the letters he wrote to the churches, he declared he was an apostle of Christ Jesus (Rom. 1:1; Eph. 1:1; Col. 1:1; 1 Tim. 1:1; 2 Tim. 1:1; and Titus 1:1). The apostle James also knew who he was: "James, a servant of God and of the Lord Jesus Christ" (James 1:1).

Though Paul was in chains while writing the book of Philippians, he talked about joy and rejoicing numerous times. How could he do that? These apostles in the New Testament knew who they were, declared their value through Jesus Christ, and changed the world. They were beaten and abandoned, and they suffered and died cruel deaths. But they experienced joy. James declared it right at the beginning of his letter: "Dear brothers and sisters, when troubles of any kind come your way, consider it an opportunity for great joy" (James 1:2 NLT). Seriously? How could James say that? Because he knew whose he was. He knew his purpose, and it was greater than his problems.

Even Jesus, the Son of God, knew his purpose and who he was. Before Jesus went to the cross, he had an intimate conversation with his father, declaring his purpose while

---

43. Used with permission from Candace Giesbrecht.

he walked on this earth: "For you granted him authority over all people that he might give eternal life to all those you have given him … I have brought you glory on earth by finishing the work you gave me to do" (John 17:2, 4). You and I need reminding that we don't live in a chaotic, random world. We don't need to wonder when the dailyness of life will swallow us up. We belong to the one who created the earth and planned for you and me to be here at this time and place in the history of the world. It's not random; there is divine purpose.

To whom do you belong? Do you belong to your husband, children, career, or even church? Why not ask God to help you figure it out? I believe that God loves it when we call out to him and lean into his unending grace. The Bible promises, "You make known to me the path of life; you will fill me with joy in your presence, with eternal pleasures at your right hand" (Ps. 16:11).

TAKING HOLD OF BEAUTY

As a speaker and writer, it gives me enormous pleasure when I can guide others to find their value and purpose. It's especially rewarding to help young children and teenagers. In 2019, I had an unusual opportunity to minister to young people in the country of Colombia.

In February 2019, I had the ultimate joy of travelling to Colombia with two friends on the Women Together team, Margaret Gibb and Carol Ann Hurtubise. Along with our translators and drivers, for two weeks we toured this majestic country and spoke in three different cities. While we stayed in Chiquinquira, we met with Pastor Wendy Cortazar Ortiz and missionary Darren McCrea, who over the past years sought God's favour to have access to the schools in this city. What a privilege and joy for our team to speak in these schools about God's love to 1,200 children from grades 6 to 11. My focus was on grade 10, and my topic was "You are God's masterpiece."

A week earlier, while we were in Bogota, I was drawn to a young woman who created magnificent beaded, colourful, and layered necklaces and was selling them at a sidewalk market. I bought a multicoloured necklace and during my time speaking at these schools I wore it and pointed it out to the students. I said, "See this multicoloured necklace I'm wearing? It was made by a teenager just like you. She strung every bead, and she knows every detail of her masterpiece creation." Then I asked the classroom, "What do you like to create?" Lively discussion followed, and when I felt they had grasped the concept of the word "masterpiece," I gave them God's Word: "For we are God's masterpiece. He has created us anew in Christ Jesus, so we can do the good things he planned for us long ago" (Eph. 2:10 NLT).

The students understood what it meant—they are God's unique creation. I affirmed that they are a magnum opus, which is considered to be the greatest work of a person's career or a work of outstanding creativity, skill, profundity, or workmanship. At their young age, these students had their whole future ahead of them, and I'm not sure they fully grasped the extent of their value. I pray that my words planted seeds of future greatness. If we are ever going to experience the fullness of joy, we must know the magnitude and magnificence of our value and God-given purpose.

After almost three decades of teaching and speaking to women, it breaks my heart when I clearly see that we still struggle with low self-esteem and lack of worth. Oh, if I could do CPR on all women I meet and breathe God's magnificence into their souls! Instead, we need to let God's *rhema*—his living, breathing word of life in the Bible—magnify our value and purpose.

JESUS VALUES WOMEN

During Jesus's time in history, a woman's place and value came from bearing and raising children and running a home. Christ never hesitated in breaking barriers to give people hope and point people to their full potential. Our acceptance is not based on our performance, culture, or tradition, but our value is in Christ.

There are many examples of women in the New Testament who had an important role in Jesus's ministry or who were offered a second chance through the compassion of Christ:

- Mary was the first woman to see Jesus after the resurrection (John 20:1–18).
- Jesus did not condemn the woman caught in adultery; instead he told her, "Go now and leave your life of sin" (John 8:11).
- Jesus travelled and proclaimed the good news with "women who had been cured of evil spirits and diseases: Mary (called Magdalene) from whom seven demons had come out … and many others" (Luke 8:2–3).
- Jesus stood up for women and protected them. When Mary took a pint of expensive perfume and poured it on Jesus's feet and was condemned by Judas, Jesus defended Mary and said, "Leave her alone" (John 12:7).
- Jesus went out of his way to meet women at their greatest point of need. The woman at the well fetched water during the hottest part of the day so she would not feel the village women's condemnation. Yet Jesus offered to give her what she needed most: living water (John 4:10).

I love what T. D. Jakes says in his book *Power for Living:* "We are not valuable because we love God; we are valuable because He loves us."[44] We know our value and become joyful when we know we are the work of God instead of always focusing on our work for God.

---

44. T. D. Jakes, *Power for Living* (Shippensburg: Destiny Image Publishers, 2009), 112.

GROW YOUR JOY

We have to fight to make joy a daily reality and choose to be warriors for truth against all the negative mind games the enemy wants to throw at us. I urge you, dear reader, to guard your heart to protect your value and then respect yourself the way Christ respected all women.

1. Treat yourself with tender care. Once I discovered the value of my putter, I treated it with tender loving care. I protected its value by buying a head cover and new grip. Discovering our value is not a one-time realization or event. We have to dig in and then protect it.

We can become confident women who can have victory and joy in spite of our messes, disappointments, and failures. I love what my author friend Debbie Taylor Williams shares in her book *The Plan A Woman in a Plan B World:*

> My most joy-filled moments are those spent abiding with Christ, being in his presence doing the things to which Christ has called me. Whether we are taking care of our family, ministering to those in need, or living for Christ at the office, his joy abides within us when we intentionally abide in him by following his will and ways. Jesus is faithful to his promise: "If you keep My commandments, you will abide in My love; just as I have kept My Father's commandments and abide in His love. These things I have spoken to you so that My joy may be in you, and that your joy may be made full" (John 15:10–11 NASB).[45]

We all want to be happy. We work very hard at being happy. We want to look happy and have a happy story, and even if we're not happy, we're content to "fake it until we make it." We're all supposed to be having the time of our lives. We want to be like everyone else on Instagram and Facebook with their big smiles and hands waving in the air, taking part in the most fun and outrageous adventures with all our happy family and friends. We're addicted to wanting to be happy. But we need to get beyond happy because happy is very fleeting.

Remember, our joy is already inside of us. Knowing our value and experiencing sustaining joy is accessible through abiding in Christ. Joy is an inside job and is not dependent on our surroundings.

So how do we abide? Hour by hour let Jesus be our wisdom, our treasure, and our life flow. We cannot have joy through our own effort; it is through drinking from him, eating his words, resting in him, drawing strength from him, staying in his presence, and trusting him to meet all our needs. Joy also comes through asking forgiveness for ongoing sin and through specific requests. Jesus said, "You haven't tried this before, but begin now.

---

45. Debbie Taylor Williams, *The Plan A Woman in a Plan B World* (Abilene: Leafwood Publishers, 2010), 223.

Ask, using my name, and you will receive, and your cup of joy will overflow" (John 16:24 TLB). Why ask? Because joy is a fruit of the Spirit, and it's ours for the asking.

2. Become an unstoppable force. My putter has become the most reliable piece of equipment in my golf bag. Among golfers there is a saying, "Drive for show, putt for dough." Great putting is what separates the hackers from the real players. In our own lives we can go for the big adventures, the big shows, the mind-boggling latest purchases and gimmicks. But at the end of the day, knowing the significance of our value is what counts. That's pure gold.

Once you grasp the concept that you are indeed God's masterpiece and his valuable, unique creation, you will be an unstoppable force living out your full potential and being a world changer. You'll be that sought out and outstanding player in this kingdom where joy is your inheritance. Add to that,

- Your boundaries will be more loving, definitive, and stronger.
- You will stop trying to be a perfectionist or martyr and ease up on people-pleasing tendencies.
- You will have fewer expectations and will be more fun to be around.
- You will learn more about your priorities and values.
- Your goals will begin to line up with God's desires.
- Your confidence will skyrocket.
- Jealousy, comparison, and gossiping will be things of the past.
- You will feel less defensive.
- You will make better decisions.
- You won't sweat the small stuff.
- You will not harbour resentment and will be quick to forgive.
- You will intentionally make more time to abide in God.
- You will be more joyful.

There is nothing more beautiful than a woman who knows she is loved by her heavenly Father and who knows her God-given value and purpose. You already have everything you need inside of you to fulfill your glorious purpose and to give you unending joy. May that woman be you.

AND ASK GOD TO MAKE YOU JOYFUL

Ask God, Would you show me where I find my value?

S—Scripture: "For we are God's masterpiece. He has created us anew in Christ Jesus, so we can do the good things he planned for us long ago" (Eph. 2:10 NLT).

T—Thanksgiving: Thank you for the gift of the Holy Spirit that equips the life flow of joy. Thank you, God, that my life is not a random mistake but has a fulfilling and glorious purpose. Thank you that you call me your masterpiece.

O—Observation: My whole life I've been trying to find my value through relationships, clothes, accomplishments, and competing to be better and different. Over the years, I've had fleeting moments of happiness, but often I'm left still grasping for more. I need something I can count on; I desperately need sustaining joy. Knowing who I am in Christ gives me the settled assurance that I have great value and there is purpose for me here on earth. But I need help to understand and grasp this magnificent proclamation.

P—Prayer: God, help me to see myself as your masterpiece. When I look in the mirror, many of my insecurities, flaws, and mistakes shout at me and remind me of all my shortcomings. Many days I feel insecure and weak. I truly want to grab hold of all the goodness and value you see in me so that I can live with confidence and joyful purpose. Holy Spirit, soak me in your truth of who I am in Christ. Help me to guard this splendid value and offer so that your joy will also be my joy in all its fullness. I want to overflow with joy. Help me to find the way. Thank you. Amen.

THE JOY OF BELONGING
LEARNING TO LIVE ALONE

"Snuggle in God's arms. When you are hurting, when you feel lonely, left out, rejected, let Him cradle you, comfort you, reassure you of His all-sufficient power and love." —Kay Arthur[46]

Our deepest desire is to be connected with someone who fully accepts and delights in us. We need a human with whom we can share our successes and failures and who will call forth the goodness in our hearts. Loneliness is the enemy of learning to find joy in living alone. Whether we are in a crowded room, with a group of friends, or have a spouse, we can still feel utterly alone. Our longing is for someone to smile at us or throw their arm around our shoulders and ask, "Hey, would you like to go for dinner and a movie tonight?" or "How about a golf game next week?" We ache for another human being to hold us when we weep, to belly laugh with us at something hilariously funny. Being recognized and accepted and knowing we have a special place in someone's life give us assurance we belong. Intentionally cultivating connections nourishes our joy.

We're becoming an isolated and lonely Western world. In fact, loneliness and disconnection are becoming an epidemic. Pain, nausea, emptiness, and darkness in the pit of our stomach are just some of the symptoms of acute loneliness. The *Montreal Gazette* gave a startling insight into this topic by stating, "Some scholars suggest that we

---

46. Kay Arthur, *My Savior, My Friend: A Daily Devotional* (Eugene: Harvest House Publishers, 1995).

are experiencing an "epidemic of loneliness … Indeed, research shows that around one in five Canadians experience some level of loneliness or isolation."[47]

Never before have we had more connections through social media and instant information, but we've become a lonely generation. Tara John wrote an article in the *Times* entitled "How the World's First Loneliness Minister Will Tackle 'the Sad Reality of Modern Life,'" which noted, "A 2010 survey suggested more than a third of American citizens over the age of 45 feel lonely … Young people aren't immune either. The U.K.'s Office for National Statistics (ONS) found that 16 to 24 year-olds reported feeling more lonely than pensioners between the ages of 65 to 74."[48]

We've become so slick in our technology that we no longer need each other. ATM machines, self-checkouts and of course the Internet and social media are all taking away desired and needed human connection. In fact, we've become so isolated and independent there is a new term for our aloneness: *self-partnered*. What does that mean? *Self-partnered* is an alternative for the word *single* as a relationship status. It declares we don't have to rely on anyone in this world to give us love and approval.

Really?

We are made for intimate human connection, and if we don't have that relatedness in a marriage, workplace, or family, we can feel utterly alone. Above all, without question, God needs to be the lover of our souls and the one we look to for everything. But while we're still human, we need hugs, words of encouragement, and someone to look us in the eyes and tell us, "God made someone special when he made you."

WE'RE MADE TO BE CONNECTED

To overcome or accept our aloneness, it is vital to our soul to know we have a connection with someone who *gets us*. No one understands this or *gets us* more profoundly than Jesus. Jesus, the Son of God, is part of the trinity, the holy family of Father, Son, and Holy Spirit. All three are deeply connected in ways we will probably never understand. That is a complete picture of a divine, intimate, and perfect relationship. But this I know: You and I are made in God's image, and because we have the DNA of our creator, we are made for connection, a supernatural connection only heaven can provide.

Larry Crabb in his book *Connecting* sums this up so well:

We were fashioned by a God whose deepest joy is connection with himself, a God who created us to enjoy the pleasure he enjoys by connecting supremely with him but also with each other. To experience the joy of connection is life; to

---

47. Victoria Carmichael, "An Epidemic of Loneliness Threatens Canadians' Health," *Montreal Gazette*, May 16, 2018. Available at https://montrealgazette.com/opinion/opinion-an-epidemic-of-loneliness-threatens-canadians-health.

48. Tara John, "The World's First Loneliness Minister."

not experience it is death to our souls, death to our deepest desires, death to everything that makes us human.[49]

Connection is where we find our meaning and power and our joy, as it is rooted in the intimate connection with God and his kingdom. And no one *gets us* like Jesus. He knows what we're going through. Jesus was deeply touched by other people's sadness and suffering, and in many places the Bible comments that Jesus had compassion. "When the Lord saw her, his heart went out to her and he said, 'Don't cry'" (Luke 7:13).

We may have a marriage contract or a business arrangement that we thought would define us and make us feel connected. We want connections, not contracts. Connection happens when we identify with another entity. Our first and most vital life-giving bond comes from God, who sent his son Jesus to come to earth to love us with a sacrificial love. Secondly, in connecting with others we begin to nourish our soul and experience life on earth in all its fullness. Kay Warren in *Choose Joy* gives great insight:

> What a gift we give to each other when we receive into our hands and our hearts somebody else's feelings. People are dying to be listened to. People are dying to be able to pour out their hearts and not be judged, not be told they're crazy, not be told their feelings don't matter … Remember, nothing will restore joy in another person's heart faster than the words, "I accept you as you are."[50]

When we're connected to God and one another, we may be alone, but we don't feel lonely. The Holy Spirit is in us to help us know we're connected and to help us live with power. When the Spirit of God is alive in us, we are connected and assured of God's dynamite power. Not only that, but we have the certainty we are now part of a family, adopted into God's family. "In love he predestined us for adoption to sonship through Jesus Christ, in accordance with his pleasure and will" (Eph. 1:4–5).

Loneliness is horror, but joy is found in connecting with God. These are all nice and meaningful words, but how does this actually work? After Jack's death and my relentless pursuit to reclaim my joy, I was determined not to be lonely. I knew it was vital to my soul to stay connected. Prior to Jack's death, I'd never experienced loneliness. I'd been married since I was 19, had my children, and always had a fulfilling career. Feeling alone or lonely was never part of my experience. Until three weeks after Jack's funeral.

It was Jack's and my custom to meet every morning at 6:20 to read the Bible and pray together sitting side by side in our custom-made traditional plaid prayer chairs. One morning while sitting alone in my chair, I grasped the harsh reality that Jack's chair was

---

49. Crabb, *Connecting*, 55.
50. Warren, *Choose Joy*, 178, 176.

empty and he would never sit in it again. Not only that, but it had snowed the previous night, and through our big picture window I eyed our barbecue and patio furniture covered in snow. Everything was different and surreal. Negative words whirled in my head. *I will never see him use that barbecue again. Never again will we all sit around that big patio table. Now I'm the one who has to shovel the snow off the deck. He will never again sit in his beloved wing chair.*

At that moment I felt *alone* and excruciatingly *lonely*. It left me gasping for air, and I wailed like a beaten dog. I was startled when my phone rang and the caller identification was the name of a dear friend, Joanne Bonk. After my initial "hello" all you could hear were my sobs. I waited for a response but realized the silence was because my dear friend was crying with me.

Once I finished that harrowing phone call, I made a declaration. I was not going to be a *lonely* widow. I was smart enough to know it would take daily choices to, first of all, stay connected to God and make him my priority and then nurture rich and loving relationships with other people. If I wanted my life to be meaningful and joyful and to be part of a tribe or community, it was up to me to make it happen.

It's a harsh reality, but it's the truth. If we want to receive love, we have to give it. If we want people to listen to us, we have to be willing to listen to them. To receive we have to pour out. The Bible gives us so many examples of how to be connected and stay in loving relationships. Here are just a few samples:

- *Love.* "Finally, all of you, be like-minded, be sympathetic; love one another, be compassionate and humble" (1 Pet. 3:8).
- *Comfort.* "Our Lord Jesus Christ, the Father of compassion and the God of all comfort, who comforts us in all our troubles, so that we can comfort those in any trouble with the comfort we ourselves receive from God" (2 Cor. 1:3–4).
- *Accept.* "Accept one another, then, just as Christ accepted you" (Rom. 15:7).
- *Forgive.* "Be kind and compassionate to one another, forgiving each other, just as in Christ God forgave you" (Eph. 4:32).
- *Pray.* "Therefore confess your sins to each other and pray for each other so that you may be healed" (James 5:16).

Some of my richest experiences and connections have been birthed by praying for and with other people or having others pray for me. When I asked my group of prayer warriors to pray for my "if only" (see chapter 3), I bared my soul and by doing so let them into my most vulnerable places. When we humble ourselves and allow the Holy Spirit to flow through us by admitting our needs to others, declaring God's promise, and seeking hope, an invisible thread connects our hearts and nourishes trust and friendship.

FOSTERING VULNERABILITY

Overcoming loneliness awaits our admission of "I need you." It expresses our inability to do life alone and our desire to find joy through connecting with other people. Humbling ourselves to admit we need each other demands vulnerability. I'm not saying it's easy. I can't tell you how often I've heard "Vulnerability sounds wonderful, but it's not for me. Nope, I don't do vulnerability." We have to understand that vulnerability is not airing our laundry or letting it all hang out. Over the years, I've found that when I open my heart and give someone else access to my feelings and stories, it gives permission for the other person to do likewise.

Brené Brown talks a lot about vulnerability in her book *Daring Greatly*. I admire the way she addresses this topic.

> Vulnerability is based on mutuality and requires boundaries and trust. It's not oversharing, it's not purging, it's not indiscriminate disclosure, and it's not celebrity-style social media information dumps. Vulnerability is about sharing our feelings and our experiences with people who have earned the right to hear them.[51]

Yes, we can go it alone, *self-partner,* and tell ourselves we're fine, we don't need anyone. I am woman, hear me roar. We've been hurt too many times and are not doing it again. But I want none of us to end up like Christopher McCandless, an Emory University graduate who became fed up with society, travelled the country without any money, and made a trip to Alaska. I saw the movie *Into the Wild*, a story of how Christopher McCandless thought he would find joy and fulfillment by isolating himself in Alaska. Sadly, he slowly died, either from starvation or from eating poisonous food. He died alone, and his words "Happiness is only real when shared" were one of his last journal entries. I hated the end of that movie. It drilled into my spirit that if we want joy we need to make ourselves vulnerable and realize we need a hand to pull us up.

But vulnerability can be a terrifying word. To become vulnerable we have to believe we are worthy of love and begin to nurture a relationship where there is trust. We need hugs, affirmation, someone to weep with us and share our joy. If we have these life-giving relationships in our life, we can live alone, but we won't feel lonely.

WE LONG TO BELONG

The search for community and belonging is a fundamental life quest. The woman at the well fetched water at the hottest time of the day when no one else was around because she felt she did not belong or fit in with the rest of society. After Jesus offered her the gift

---

51. Brené Brown, *Daring Greatly: How the Courage to Be Vulnerable Transforms the Way We Live, Love, Parent and Lead* (New York: Penguin Group, 2015), 45.

of living water, she ran into the village to tell people about the man who offered her hope and life (John 4:4–29). She had been accepted and felt a new belonging.

Growing up, it felt like we simply belonged. It felt natural, like we didn't have to work to belong in different communities. We had church friends and our extended family and walked around the neighbourhood in the evening chatting about gardens, the latest news, or crabgrass. Today, I believe people long for that *front porch* experience. Joseph R. Myers in his book *The Search To Belong* explains it this way: "The porch further fostered a sense of community and neighborliness. In the evenings, as people moved outdoors, the porch served to connect individuals. The neighbors from next door might stop by one's house, to sit on the porch and discuss both personal and community issues."[52]

Sadly, over time, garage door openers and air conditioners lured us inside, and we no longer shout "hello" to our neighbours walking down the street or share the latest national news or neighbourhood gossip. We want to belong somewhere to someone, but it gets harder all the time. With many people working from home, tall fences separating our houses, and with YouTube showing us how to do everything ourselves, we no longer need each other.

I know many lonely single women. So often I hear: "If only I was married…" Many singles believe they will have ultimate joy when they belong to someone in a marriage relationship. But marriage has no guarantee that it will fulfill all your needs. I also know many women who are achingly lonely in their marriages.

I've had to come to terms with my widowhood. I am alone. But I'm not lonely, because I told God I was declaring his promise that he was my husband. Sound strange? Here is my dearest friend Shaunie Brown's story how she also came to accept her singleness by acknowledging God as her husband:

Will I always be alone? Will I ever get married? I know God is always with me, but I need a human beside me. Those thoughts and questions tormented me, and I could not find peace with my singleness. The straw that broke the camel's back was when an individual looked into my eyes and asked, "Are you married yet?" "What's wrong with you?" "I hear you are very picky." Their questions pierced my heart and spiralled me into a place of deeper loneliness and angst.

God redeemed those questions with a deep longing to find a resolution. In my heart, I knew there was an answer. My daily prayers were focused on seeking resolve: "God, if you are who you say you are, please reveal yourself to me." With fervency I searched his word for direction and answers. My prayer life intensified with a determination to come to grips with my singlehood. In my heart, I knew I had to come to a place where being alone didn't matter.

In my quest for truth I was overwhelmed with the Father's desire to have a loving and intimate relationship with me. I began to see him as a father who longs to communicate with me and care for me. He desires to share his perfect love in a tangible way that is greater than any human being could offer me. Isaiah 54:5 became alive to me: "For your Maker is your husband—the LORD Almighty is his name—the Holy One of Israel is your Redeemer; he is called the God of all the earth." Isaiah 62:4: "No longer will they call you Deserted, or name your land Desolate. But you will be called Hephzibah, and your land Beulah [Hebrew for 'married']." I recall sitting and weeping. Finally I had my answer. God, my Father, through his Holy Spirit, revealed himself to me with a powerful truth. Through his living word he gave me the settled assurance that it didn't matter what my state of being was—married or single. He would be my everything. He was enough!

It was February 14, 1993—a day etched in my mind forever. The divine revelation and understanding of God as my father and as a husband sustained me and gave me the ability to say, "No matter what, I know I am never alone. He is always with me!" He will care for me as no other human being could possibly ever do. Daily I experience unspeakable joy filled with the Father's love. Single or married, I am never alone, because I have him. He is everything I need when I need it![53]

I love Shaunie's honest and raw story because it culminated in finding that steadfast joy. Almost daily I remind God that he's my husband and I need his help with my finances and how to fix the lights that went out underneath the kitchen counter. I need someone to shovel the snow on my driveway or some feedback on my latest writing. The answers come. Just at the right time. Always.

GROW YOUR JOY

During the month of March to the middle of May 2020, two of the most crucial months of the COVID-19 pandemic, I again discovered the horror of isolation and aloneness. Throughout that time period I had not had a hug or human connection. Toward the end of May I met with a friend to do some outdoor volunteer work, with the proper two-metre physical distancing. With a big smile on my face I got out of the car to greet Joanne but was careful to keep my distance. She smiled and offered, "Heidi, come here; let me hug you." She wrapped her arms around me, and I hung on and wept. I'd been without human touch for over two months and had forgotten how desperately we need hugs.

---

53. Used with permission from Shaunie Brown.

How we're created for human connection. Isolation is not in our DNA. Our souls shrivel up without human touch.

We're made for connections and belonging, but they don't just happen. They require vulnerability, intentional effort, and time. Let's look at some ways we can grow our joy. But first, ask yourself some questions:

- Am I really alone? Or are there people I can reach out to but I haven't made the effort?
- What have I done to create relationships? Have I made myself vulnerable and put myself out there to let people know I need a friend?
- Have I joined a group where I need to keep showing up?

Here's what I've learned over the past years. To grow joy,

1. Deepen your relationship with God. Overcoming loneliness means we have to take intentional steps to move forward. In order to be filled, we have to pour out. But first of all, deepen your relationship with God. Buy interesting books on spiritual formation, read the Bible, learn to pray fervently, and get to know God, who is your father and your husband. Ask people to pray for you, and pray for others. Trust God, and believe he will help you find your connections, belonging, and purpose. It's through him that we find our fresh joy. "Though you have not seen him, you love him; and even though you do not see him now, you believe in him and are filled with an inexpressible and glorious joy" (1 Pet. 1:8).

2. Find your community. This is a harsh reality, but if you want community, you have to go out to find and build your community. That means joining a golf group or bowling team, a knitting or crocheting group, a cycling group, a book club, or best yet, a Bible study group in your local church.

My richest experiences come through facilitating a women's evening Bible study and leading a Grief Share group. I'm also part of three golf groups and speaking and writing organizations, and I'm very involved with my local church. These tribes and communities didn't just show up; I had to make them happen and say "yes." I allowed my vulnerability to speak to me so that I could confess, "Yes, I need to be connected and find a place where I belong."

3. Make time to be a friend. Many of you are blessed to be close to family. Or you may be like me and have family scattered all across North America. We all need friends, for they are the heartbeat and lifeline of our existence. They teach us how to laugh, love, and live. They show us how to escape our comfort zones and invite new possibilities. The most important gift we can give someone is our time. How do you spell love? T.I.M.E. When we give this away, we receive unwavering joy.

4. Your home is your haven. Four months after Jack's death I couldn't wait to sell my home and move into something that didn't have so many painful memories. Now I'm relieved that I followed the guidelines to wait one year before making huge decisions and that I stayed in my existing home. It's become my haven, my sanctuary, a place for me to run to after a trip or a long day away. I've made it my own, and I suggest you do this as well. I've repainted some walls and added new pictures and pillows and a bit more feminine decor. And lots of candles. Our homes are a reflection of who we are, and when we design them to fit our personality, we will find joy inviting our friends over or being alone.

5. Do what you've never done before. Use this time to do things you've always wanted to do. Now you can travel more, learn to do creative projects, take that road trip, go to that movie, enjoy that knitting course, make raspberry jam, ride a bike, write a book, or lead a Bible study. Maybe now's the time to get reacquainted with that high school friend you found on Instagram. Think how wonderful it is to eat apple crisp in bed (don't forget the ice cream) and watch your favourite movies in your pyjamas. Why not? It's OK to learn to enjoy your life.

6. Don't forget to count your blessings. Open your gratitude journal and look at all the goodness in your life. Writing it down makes it real and it takes away the sting of feeling cast aside.

3721. I love my flannel sheets

3751. Some lovely, quiet evenings at home

3843. My house looks really nice; I love my house

3858. Laughter

3862. When I feel God's presence

3871. Walked with the sun on my face

3879. Early supper at Earls. Good food. Great company

3910. Sat in the sun on the deck for a while

This is one of the most crucial chapters in finding fresh joy. Whatever life status we're at, we'll never feel completely fulfilled and joyful until we become deeply connected with God and one another. My website is called "Heart Connections" because I believe connections are the most crucial aspects of finding joy. May you find yours.

AND ASK GOD TO MAKE YOU JOYFUL

Ask God, How can I deepen my connection with you?

S—Scripture: "Though you have not seen him, you love him; and even though you do not see him now, you believe in him and are filled with an inexpressible and glorious joy" (1 Pet. 1:8).

T—Thanksgiving: Thank you, God, for loving me in spite of the many times I fail to deepen my relationship with you. Thank you that you've always been there when I need you even though I couldn't see it. Thank you that you're always working and making a way to draw me closer into your presence and your unconditional love.

O—Observation: I receive and declare the promise that I will love God even though I cannot see him. Some days it's really hard because I need a human to hug me and show me I'm accepted and special. I recognize that in order to tap into joy, I first need to tap into God's love and acceptance.

P—Prayer: Heavenly Father, I long to pursue a deep and loving connection with you. I want the kind of depth that will plunge me into your indescribable love and fresh joy. I declare that I desire your friendship and presence but don't know how to attain it. Help me to be vulnerable to open my heart to you and the people around me who are possible friends. Vulnerability is scary. What if I get hurt and end up even more alone than I am now? Take my hand and guide me through this unknown process. Also, teach me the concept that you are my father and my husband and you will look after me and provide for me in my time of need. Help me to learn to lean into you and trust you when the future looks uncertain and lonely. Show me how to learn to live alone but not be lonely. I need you. Thank you that you're always with me. Amen.

JOY AND BEAUTY OF LIVING WATER
PITIFUL OR POWERFUL

"When the heart is full of joy, it always allows its joy to escape. It is like the fountain in the marketplace; whenever it is full it runs away in streams, and so soon as it ceases to overflow, you may be quite sure that it has ceased to be full. The only full heart is the overflowing heart." —Charles Spurgeon (1859)

One of our greatest longings is to experience pleasure. Surprisingly one of life's most captivating feelings that thoroughly delight our brain is the soothing and steady sound of running water. Science indicates that the rhythm of ocean waves and tides coming in and out can impact the rhythm of the neuronal waves in our brain, and this can result in a more peaceful pace of thought.

Companies have become successful by developing apps on our phones that manifest the sounds of ocean waves and moving water. Mysteriously we are drawn to these sounds as they invite us in to calm our mind and evoke serenity and joy.

If possible, we plan our vacations to be close to a beach or at the lake. What joy to hear the crashing and steady cadence of waves as our toes are stretched out in the sun and we're reading a riveting book or getting exercise and enjoyment from water sports like surfing, scuba diving, sailing, and swimming. How many times have we said "ahhhhh" when we've stepped into a refreshing shower or a steaming soothing bath? Water has a mystifying effect. It's an indication of a refreshing life through the steady ebb and flow of water.

Eight months after my lonely and heart-wrenching grief period of Jack's death, my dearest friends Terry and Shaunie Brown took me along on a summer road trip. Our destination: the lush vegetation of the state of Oregon and its majestic coastline. We had our sights set on Cannon Beach, and like packing horses, we lugged chairs, umbrellas, blankets, books, and outrageously delicious food to the perfect spot near the water. For two days, I felt like I'd opened the windows of heaven. I alternated between sprawling out on a comfy chair, immersing myself in a great book, and walking up and down the water's edge with water splashing against my calves. Something shifted in my soul as I gazed at the endless blue-and-white horizon and heard the rhythmic crashing of the waves. Overcome with emotion, I allowed tears to spill over with joy at the blue and turquoise colours of the waves and sounds of the water. For the first time in months, my body calmed, and I was flooded with well-being and fresh joy. These two days were some of my most healing times. How is that possible? The sound and motion of the ocean waves opened up my soul and unleashed "living water."

WATER CALMS OUR BRAINS

Being around water gives our brains a rest from the stimulation and distractions all around us. It calms us from the noise of traffic, loud conversations, sirens, planes, and the ping of our phones.

> The peaceful feeling we get at the beach could be a result of molecular changes that are happening in our bodies. The ocean's waves produce negative ions. Negative ions accelerate our body's ability to absorb oxygen. They also balance levels of serotonin; a chemical produced by the body that is related to mood and stress. This is one reason why being at the beach [has] been linked by scientists to positive mental energy and a general overall sense of health and well-being.[54]

This helps to explain the soothing and healing effect of the sound of water. Our brain is calmer and we become less anxious and are more productive and creative. It's incredible that living water actually has the ability to help us live better and healthier lives. How many of you have had great creative ideas, answers to prayer, or other revelations while in the shower?

The stories during Jesus's time took place in nations where water was a desired and precious resource. You couldn't just turn on the faucet or press a button on the fridge to draw a cool glass of fresh water. Water wells were precious, and cities and towns were built up around this desired commodity. Part of a woman's daily chore was to walk to

---

54. Rebeka Beris, "Science Explains How the Beach Can Change Our Brains and Mental Health," Lifehack.org, 2018.

the local well, draw water, and carry it back to her home. This included water for family cleansing, meals, animals, and consumption. We aren't talking about a little bit of water for a drink—it's about providing water for your family, including animals, and everything else needed to get through the day.

WATER IS LIFE-GIVING

When we read the Bible as a book we may understand the characteristics of Jesus and the Holy Spirit. However, when we look at Jesus and the Holy Spirit as a relationship, everything changes. Jesus came down from heaven so he could lift us up. He became nothing so that we can become everything. It all starts with receiving and understanding the flow and power of the Holy Spirit.

Water is life-giving, and it starts when we're born. We came out of our mothers' bodies through a slosh of living water. When a woman's "water breaks," it is time to give new birth. Our bodies are made up of 60 to 80 percent water, and water keeps our bodies hydrated and healthy.

The Bible commands us to be baptized in water when we declare our commitment to follow Jesus. It's an outward expression of an inward declaration. We're immersed in water as dying to ourselves and come out of it with the pronouncement to live for Christ. It's a profoundly intimate and hopeful image of new life. But this symbolism doesn't have any power to transform us into the likeness of Jesus Christ until we learn to draw on the life-giving water of Jesus Christ.

WHAT IS THIS LIVING WATER?

Jesus walked this earth and went through every emotion that you and I will ever experience. Betrayal, rejection, loneliness.

Jesus knows us. He gets us.

But he doesn't just get us. He wants to give us power to live this life. Jesus knew we would encounter lots of trouble while walking this earth.

Jesus offered this living water to an outcast, a Samaritan woman at Jacob's well. In Deborah Lovett's book *Gushing Springs*, she explains it this way:

> It wasn't a coincidence that Jesus came at the sixth hour. In our language, that's noon. It was extremely hot at that hour. Most women came to draw water in the cooler parts of the day, the early morning and the early evening. The Samaritan Woman, however, came at the hottest time of the day. Jesus met her when she thought she was alone and safe from the ridicule of others—at a lonely point of despair and desperation. It's just like Jesus to meet her at a

well that holds stagnant well water when He Himself is the Gushing Spring of Living Water![55]

Other people rejected the woman at the well, but not Jesus. He sent all his disciples into town to buy lunch because Jesus wanted to be alone with her. He understood her harsh and lonely life. He knew about her previous five husbands and that she was living with a sixth man. He didn't just get her. He wanted to give her new life and move her forward with new power.

When Jesus asked her for a drink, she was aghast. She was a member of the hated mixed Jewish-Samaritan race. No respectable Jewish man would talk to a woman under these circumstances. So she asked, "How can you ask me for a drink?" (John 4:9). I love the way Jesus treated women, and he answered her, "If you knew the gift of God and who it is that asks you for a drink, you would have asked him and he would have given you living water" (John 4:10).

This woman, filled with shame and condemnation, was given the greatest gift any of us can ever receive. Jesus gave her living water! She was so joyful that she ran into town and proclaimed this good news: "Come, see a man who told me everything I ever did. Could this be the Messiah?" (John 4:29).

We need physical water to survive physically and spiritual living water to thrive spiritually.

PITIFUL OR POWERFUL?

We Christians have this unsurpassable power available to us. It's accessible and perpetual, and yet so many Christ followers live pitiful and fruitless lives. Before Jesus left this earth he told his disciples, "'Whoever believes in me, as the Scripture has said, rivers of living water will flow from within them.' By this he meant the Spirit, whom those who believed in him were later to receive. Up to that time the Spirit had not been given, since Jesus had not yet been glorified" (John 7:38–39).

This Holy Spirit, the living water that redeems our souls and seals our salvation, equips us to live unstoppable and fully charged powerful and joyful Christian lives. Here are just some of the extravagant gifts of the Holy Spirit:

- When we are weak he intercedes for us at the right hand of the Father (Rom. 8:26–27).
- He guides us into all truth (John 16:13).
- He is a seal guaranteeing our inheritance (Eph. 1:13–14).
- He gives us the same power that raised Christ from the dead (Eph. 1:19–20).
- He convicts us of guilt, sin, and righteousness (John 16:8).

---

55. Deborah Lovett, *Gushing Springs* (Friendswood: Baxter Press, 2005), 54.

- He fills us with all the gifts and all abilities we need (1 Cor. 12:7–11).
- He tells us what is to come (John 16:13).
- He tells us that we can do even greater things (John 14:12).
- The Spirit reveals to us the inconceivable riches that God prepared for those who love him (1 Cor. 2:9–10).
- He assures us that we can do anything (Phil. 4:13)!

Centuries before Jesus came to give us this living water, God declared that we would receive it:

- "With joy you will draw water from the wells of salvation" (Isa. 12:3).
- "For I will pour water on the thirsty land, and streams on the dry ground; I will pour out my Spirit on your offspring, and my blessings on your descendants" (Isa. 44:3).

Now that we have this living water within us, why do we often feel so joyless and powerless? We look at these promises and ask ourselves, "Why do I only get a little dribble now and then? What's stopping me from experiencing the fullness of this gushing living water?"

It's a tragedy that we're unaware of our full access to this fresh bubbling water in our souls. Instead, we drink polluted water and think it's the best it's going to get. Our self-striving, wrong motives, and doing life in our own strength and power keep us thirsty for more. It's never enough. So we keep drinking this imitation that doesn't have the power to transform us or to give us the joy and fulfillment we desperately seek.

Since becoming a Christian in 1978, I've had trickles of this living water and the occasional waterfalls. But Jesus's words give me hope, and I want the fullness, gushing, and constant daily flow. None of us can have this full indwelling of the living water while we live in this imperfect world, but it's a goal to pursue.

Also, it helps to know what's stopping the flow. We need to approach God: "Heavenly Father, I'm as thirsty as the Psalmist, who cried out, 'As the deer pants for streams of water, so my soul pants for you, my God' (Ps. 42:1). God, what is obstructing the flow of your Spirit within me so that I become completely satisfied in you?"

So what robs our fulfillment and joy? In my own search for daily empowerment God revealed two obstructions.

DIGGING OUR OWN CISTERNS

Imagine this: My long-awaited trip to the ocean has finally arrived. I'm ready to enjoy the day, and I pack up my books, chair, snacks, water, and a shovel. I set down my backpack with all my belongings, and I start digging, hoping to find some water. Over my right shoulder is the vast ocean with its turquoise water glistening as the waves roll in and out. Eventually I'm sweating, but I keep digging and hoping. I've come all this way, and surely I'll soon find water.

Sounds ridiculous. Right?

Maybe that's your and my story, and we don't even realize it. How often have we thirsted for pleasure, accomplishments, or the right relationship and are worn out from all our digging? Or how about manipulating opportunities, working into the midnight hours, and pushing open doors that aren't ready to be opened? Often we come away exhausted, disappointed, and emptier than before. Many of us are people pleasers, hoping we'll finally be acknowledged as good and smart enough that we'll feel loved and accepted. We keep digging, and surely some day we'll find that ultimate fulfillment.

But Jesus didn't say, "Hey, keep digging; one day you'll find what you're looking for."

For centuries, people have dug their own cisterns, instead of turning to God for their redemption and living water. God used the prophet Jeremiah to warn his people to turn away from their worthless idols and religious systems and return to him. Jeremiah declared these words for the Lord: "For my people have done two evil things: They have abandoned me—the fountain of living water. And they have dug for themselves cracked cisterns that can hold no water at all!" (Jer. 2:13 NLT). God beckoned his people to come to him instead of digging around for water in their unreliable, broken, and dirty cisterns.

Why would anyone turn away from a fresh, sparkling spring of water and turn to a dirty collection of rainwater? Because we all thirst for something. Our soul becomes dry and parched, and we try everything to fill our empty void. We push ourselves yet deny that we're workaholics, perfectionists, and overachievers.

We dig and dig.

Feel overwhelmed.

Are anxious and don't sleep.

Get depressed.

Get up and start all over again.

We wonder if living water is real, because it sounds like an unattainable myth. So we keep digging away, and sadly we don't even realize we're building our own cisterns.

Kay Warren in her book *Choose Joy* talks about cisterns. I like what she says: "The problem is that the cisterns you and I dig don't hold enough water to get us through the tough times. They crack and run dry. Rather than turning to God we just dig a little harder. We drag ourselves out day after day looking for joy in the same place that didn't bring joy the day before."[56]

My hard-working German parents raised me to be innovative and constructive and just "get 'er done." To get a "well done" or "atta girl" from my dad meant having to show

---

56. Warren, *Choose Joy*, 79.

some sweat on my brow. So I learned. To work hard. Overachieve. For years, I had a full-time career and a ministry, and yet I was also a pastor's wife, a mom and stepmom of a blended family, and very involved in my home church. I loved it, but looking back, I didn't realize how often I drew water from a cracked and leaky cistern.

After Jack died, I was bereft, exhausted with grief, and without energy. Hoping just to survive each day. It wrecked me to cancel an entire year of prebooked speaking engagements and travel arrangements. I had no other option but to draw on the "living water" that Jesus offers so freely.

At first it was scary. But I pressed in, and at the start of each day I prayed, "God, without you I can do nothing. Fill me with your Spirit, your life-giving living water, to heal me, restore me, and give me strength for this day." Over time, as I regained my strength, I added this to my prayer: "God, please open doors for speaking engagements. Give me opportunities to pour your love onto a broken and hurting world."

Slowly God's living water restored my soul, and I was able to travel and speak across North America and eventually into Romania and Colombia. I didn't have to bang on any doors. God opened the right speaking opportunity at the perfect time. When I thought God had abandoned me and there were blank spots on my calendar, those dates were open for a reason. It made me available to look after my grandchildren or visit with my brother-in-law David, who had stage four cancer. God's living water and timing are always spot on. Always.

Yes, we're thirsty, but God is the only source of our living water and our joy. Everything else is just a temporary fake substitute. His fresh spring of water will never run out or run dry.

LOGJAMS

While we live in this sinful world, with all of our insecurities and temptations, unknowingly we develop logjams. Logjams are old trees or branches that have fallen into a stream of water and lessen or stop the flow. That's what causes the obstructions in flowing springs of water in the physical world. In the spiritual world our logjams show up in the most unusual and unexpected places. Over time, we build many logjams. I will deal with six of them.

1. Pride. Pride is so ugly that Carey Nieuwhof in his book *Didn't See It Coming* dedicated an entire chapter to this topic. He says that pride kills: "Pride will snuff out your empathy, stifle your compassion, create division, suffocate love, foster jealousy, deaden your soul, and make you think all this is normal. It can turn you into the kind of person you loathe."[57] It makes us compare, criticize, judge, and feel superior, and over time it will

---

57. Carey Nieuwhof, *Didn't See It Coming: Overcoming the Seven Greatest Challenges That No One Expects and Everyone Experiences* (New York: Waterbrook, 2018), 117–118.

harden our heart. The Bible says, "Pride goes before destruction, a haughty spirit before a fall" (Prov. 16:18). The logjam of pride quickly turns a living stream into a little trickle. Drip, drip, drip, and we wonder why God "isn't coming through" for us.

2. Resentment. This is a logjam disguised with a plastic smile. It says, "Everything's fine. I'm OK." Inwardly, our soul burns with anger or offences and drinks from the poisonous well of unforgiveness, wishing the other person would die. We will never know the fullness of Jesus's gift of living water if we don't obey the command to "Be kind and compassionate to one another, forgiving each other, just as in Christ God forgave you" (Eph. 4:32). Forgiveness is never optional, but it's shocking how often we hang on to resentment. Forgiveness removes the logjam and opens the heart to receive living water. (See the epilogue for steps to forgiveness.)

3. Fear, worry, and anxiety. When was the last time all your worrying produced your desired result? What a waste of precious sleep and energy! These debilitating emotions sabotage our freedom and cause missed opportunities. After 40 years of wandering in the desert, the Israelites did not get to see their promised land, because they feared the unknown and did not trust God. These wasteful feelings vandalize God-given opportunities and stop the flow of creativity and peace.

4. Believing Satan's lies. The apostle Paul warns us, "For our struggle is not against flesh and blood, but against the rulers, against the authorities, against the powers of this dark world and against the spiritual forces of evil in the heavenly realms" (Eph. 6:12). Believing the enemy's lies that we're not smart enough, good enough, or competent enough blocks the flow of living water. When we focus on the lies of Satan, we can't hear the voice of God helping us to live our very best life.

5. A critical, judgmental, and self-righteous spirit. I've lumped these together as they all flow out of a self-righteous spirit. It's all about you. Carey Nieuwhof in *Didn't See It Coming* describes it this way: "A judgmental attitude springs directly from the noxious well of superiority because to stay ahead, you have to invent reasons why others are behind."[58] You push people out of the spotlight because you have the need to be right and to be celebrated. Strangely enough, this arrogant attitude comes from an insecure heart that feels unloved and undervalued but manifests itself as an ugly, superior Pharisee logjam.

6. Shame. Many people are unaware that shame creates a huge logjam and keeps them trapped in their past mistakes and self-disgust. When our human need to feel loved, valued, acknowledged, heard, and protected is not met, we receive shame in our spirit. *There must be something wrong with me. I must be damaged goods. I don't belong. I feel all wrong. I just want to fade into a wall or fall through a crack.* Satan uses

---

58. Nieuwhof, *Didn't See It Coming*, 125.

our vulnerability and shameful lies to remind us how pitiful we are. Surrendering our shame and seeing ourselves under the light of God's promises of who we are in him removes those toxic logjams.

The first step to removing those logjams is to recognize and name them. Refuse to let the logjams stop the flow of life-giving water. Christ died to set you free from self-deprecating lies and the deceit of the enemy. The Bible confirms this: "It is for freedom that Christ has set us free. Stand firm, then, and do not let yourselves be burdened again by a yoke of slavery" (Gal. 5:1).

Stop the logjams from enslaving you. Take each log and ask God to help you remove it, giving access to the power and freedom of the living water. It's free for the asking. "To the thirsty I will give water without cost from the spring of the water of life" (Rev. 21:6). Christ died to set us free and gave us living water so that we can live the abundant life. To be refreshed and renewed. To unleash and experience fresh life-giving joy.

GROW YOUR JOY

1. We can have joy in all circumstances. The apostle Paul was beaten and jailed, worked to exhaustion, and went without sleep and food, and yet he declared, "Our hearts ache, but at the same time we have the joy of the Lord" (2 Cor. 6:10 TLB). How is that possible? Did you notice that he said he had "the joy of the Lord"? Not the joy of circumstances or success or a project or a plan that worked out the way he hoped. He drew on the living joy that was within him. He drew on it by choosing it.

2. You want the Niagara Falls of joy. You may love and agree with what I've written about logjams, but until you intentionally remove them, the living water cannot flow freely. Here's the unsettling part: Often we've become so comfortable with those logs that we don't even recognize them, because sin can feel pretty good. So how can we recognize something as wrong when it still feels so right? We've lived with those feelings for so long that we don't recognize them as being harmful and stopping the flow of joy. Ask God to help reveal your logjams. Then pray and ask him to help you remove them. You don't want just droplets of joy; you want the Niagara Falls of refreshing joy. It's yours for the asking.

3. Know we are unique because of the living water. In the devotional book that I continue to read over and over called *The One Year Hearing His Voice Devotional*, Chris Tiegreen makes these great statements: "We aren't distinguished from the world because of our moral code or our theology; we are unique because God lives in us and with us and shares His heart with us. We live by revelation, not by principles. We are guided, not self-directed. We are immersed in a relationship, not an ideology."[59]

---

59. Chris Tiegreen, *Hearing His Voice: 365 Days of Intimate Communication With God* (Bonita Springs: Tyndale House Publishers, 2014), 169.

As Christians we are unique and have something the rest of the world longs for—instant access to unexplainable power. We can have this in a single thought. You see, our minds can only process one thought at a time. When we're spiralling into despair or a temptation that lures us, we can stop and change the words in our head. Instead of thinking "This is hard and hopeless. I'll never get through this," we can change the words to "God, you're alive and flowing through me right now. I have everything I need to get through this, and I trust you to help me. Refresh me and help me to move forward with assurance and joy. Thank you for living in me and quenching my thirst."

What a profound reminder that we can saturate ourselves in this distinctive power available to those who know that heaven is their home and source of endless, living joy!

4. Be an overflowing fountain for others. The sweetness of our relationship with Jesus needs to overflow generously to others. We are to be fountains through which Jesus can flow as a "river of living water." In the same way that living water has been given to us, we need to splash it onto others.

In 1998, I stood near Trevi's fountain in Italy and felt the splash of droplets of water on my face. Sheer joy! We need to be those conduits for God's goodness to flow through us and splash onto people around us. It perpetuates joy. It's unexplainable, but that's how it happens.

AND ASK GOD TO MAKE YOU JOYFUL

Ask God, What is squelching the flow of my living water?

S—Scripture: "Our hearts ache, but at the same time we have the joy of the Lord" (2 Cor. 6:10 TLB).

T—Thanksgiving: What a gift to know that, in spite of my circumstances and pain, I can have joy. Thank you that I don't have to follow a six-step program to achieve this or strive for a level of competence. I only need to look to you and ask for the abundance of your living water. You are such a good, good father. Thank you for giving us such simple and wonderful tools to help us live joyfully.

O—Observation: There are days when I'm completely empty, and joy feels like a distant memory. The apostle Paul encountered endless trials and pain, and yet, because Christ lived in him, he was able to declare and access joy. In the human sense, it's unexplainable and inconceivable that I can have joy in spite of the ache in my heart. If the Bible says it is possible, then I need to know what's stopping the flow of my joy.

P—Prayer: God, it is so amazing that you have placed all the resources of heaven within me. I desperately need to tap into the abundance of your joy. Thank you for the occasional trickles, but I am thirsty and desire the gushing flow. Forgive me when I get comfortable with my life and don't recognize my sinful behaviour. I acknowledge that I am too self-focused and need your help to expose my logjams. With open hands and heart I give you every room and corner of my life and ask that you please reveal whatever is blocking the flow of living water. Let joy flow through me in such beauty and power that wherever I go the water will gush onto all the people around me. I ask and wait for you to show me my logjams so that you can help me remove them. Thank you. I know you will. Amen.

CRAZY JOY
LEARNING TO FLY UPSIDE DOWN

"The Bible teaches that true joy is formed in the midst of the difficult seasons of life." —Francis Chan[60]

For three hours, our friendly Spanish-speaking driver thrust his little vehicle through the endless hairpin turns of the Pescardero Pass, known as the Grand Canyon of Colombia. Our final destination was Bucaramanga, Colombia, where our Women Together team would conduct leadership conferences, speak to social workers, and teach at churches.

To everyone's annoyance I couldn't control my gasping during the endless twisting and turning on the one-lane highway while our vehicle was sandwiched between buses and semis. As I looked down at my white-knuckled hands and then over to my translator Sally beside me, whose face was grey with beads of sweat, anxious thoughts were running through my mind. *Oh God, I hope she doesn't throw up. God, this horrific traffic and the never-ending turns are insane. Please keep us safe.*

This was crazy! We were in magnificent country, yet with all this frenetic driving I lost the inclination to look at the rugged and intense beauty of the mountains. Then I saw the sign "Bucaramanga—13 kilometres," and my heart stopped pounding. For the first time in those hair-raising three hours my breathing regulated and I calmed down. As we slowed down, I finally looked up and saw the majestic and rugged landscape of Colombia greeting me with joy.

---

60. Francis Chan, *Crazy Love: Overwhelmed by a Relentless God* (Colorado Springs: David C. Cook, 2013), 143.

I've navigated through enough nail-biting and stressful periods in my life to recognize that the state of crazy does not invite joy. Sure, there's skydiving, bungee jumping, skiing off black diamond cliffs, or mountain repelling adventures, but those give temporary jolts of excitement and pleasure. Sustainable joy is cultivated, not jolted.

CALM OR CRAZY

My ministry called Heart Connection is focused on helping women identify their present struggles so that I can clarify their needs and connect them to their source of hope and joy. I love to guide them to the relentless love of their heavenly Father and all the resources available to them. We don't live in the perfect, sinless Garden of Eden or in an illusion of an earthly heaven. So while we live in the middle of this tension we have the daily freedom to choose to grow in joy or to refuse and reject this pleasurable commodity.

At some of my conferences, as a fun and enlivening exercise, I put up two whiteboards. On one whiteboard I write "CALM" and on the other "CRAZY." Then I ask women to come up and write a word on each board about how it feels when life is calm and when life is crazy. The reality of the words always bring awareness, and sometimes the results are quite shocking. Under the heading of "CALM" the words are quite predictable, and they always make me smile.

Confident
Joyful
Bring it on
Energized
Focused
Feel connected
Happy
Strong
Secure

Those are just some feelings we enjoy when we don't try to cram too many things into our day, when we're not burnt out from living up to everyone's expectations or feeling responsible for things that are not ours to carry. We enjoy this calm when we've laid our day's agenda and worries at the foot of the cross, knowing that Jesus will guide us through the day.

Then my heart gets wrecked when I walk over to the board and see the words in the "CRAZY" column.

Hopeless
Tired

Anxious

Overwhelmed

Joyless

Suicidal

Depressed

Alone

Empty

Sadly, I discover that most women in the room identify with the crazy column instead of the calm. Is all this hyperactivity producing the good fruit of joy we desire? Are we so obsessed with feeling good that we're heading down the wrong paths and spinning out of control? Have we convinced ourselves that we can survive on four hours sleep yet tell ourselves we're not workaholics or perfectionists?

As I study the statistics, I'm no longer shocked by the downward spiral of running on empty. The *National Post* gave some interesting insight:

> With new surveys showing alarming rates of anxiety, it's a wonder we haven't all crawled under weighted blankets. A recent poll of 1,500 Canadians found 41 per cent of those surveyed identified themselves as "someone who struggles with anxiety." A third said they had been formally diagnosed with anxiety. A similar proportion had been prescribed antidepressants.[61]

Instead of seeking the free gift of calm through peace, hope, and joy from God, we're buying anxiety apps, glass beads, magnetic bracelets, and recreational marijuana. We're so desperate to feel good that we end up feeling bad. We've forgotten to put our daily hope in God, "who richly provides us with everything for our enjoyment" (1 Tim. 6:17).

Do we hope that one day all our dreams will come true, we'll have more money than we can ever spend, and we can snap our fingers to get whatever we desire? Then we'll find the fullness of joy, right? The Bible says, "This is the day the Lᴏʀᴅ has made. We will rejoice and be glad in it" (Ps. 118:24 NLT). How can we stop this pathway of crazy and learn to rejoice in each day?

WE WANT IT ALL

Friends and acquaintances on Facebook and Instagram seem to have it all, so why can't you? King Solomon had it all and should have been the happiest person on earth. He was Bill Gates, Warren Buffett, Mark Zuckerberg, and Jeff Bezos all rolled into one. World leaders, kings, and queens came to sit at King Solomon's feet and went away amazed.

---

61. Sharon Kirkey, "Nearly Half of Canadians Report Struggling With Anxiety, But Are We Really Coming Undone?" *National Post*, October 29, 2018.

On the queen of Sheba's visit, she was breathless with awe of all of King Solomon's wealth and wisdom, and she exclaimed, "In fact, I had not heard the half of it! Your wisdom and prosperity are far beyond what I was told" (1 Kings 10:7 NLT). King Solomon had it all—700 wives, 300 concubines, 12,000 horses, and wealth and other livestock as far as the eye could see. He was famous far and wide and known for his exquisite building projects, for writing 3,000 proverbs and 1,005 songs, and for building the temple in Jerusalem.

Every wish was his command, and he lacked nothing. Like most of us he started out on the right foot, by asking God for only one thing: wisdom. He confessed to God that he was only a child who did not know how to carry out the duties of the king, so he requested, "Give your servant a discerning heart to govern your people and to distinguish between right and wrong" (1 Kings 3:9). God graciously granted King Solomon his desire, and the king became one of the wisest men on earth. So where did it go awry, and when is it all enough?

John D. Rockefeller, at one time the richest man in America, was asked when enough was enough. His answer was "Just a little bit more." I truly believe that we earnestly start with the right mindset or intention, but greed, power, and a "not enough" mentality takes us on a dizzy winding road to crazy. What happened to King Solomon is that he began to enjoy God's blessings more than he enjoyed his relationship with God.

Just a little bit more is what turns our desires into bondage. Just a little bit more in my closet, garage, and bank account. Just a little bit more is what causes families to fall apart as husbands and wives work into the midnight hours, disintegrate mealtimes, break down communication, and make everything meaningless. After King Solomon's crazy ride he concluded, "When I surveyed all that my hands had done and what I had toiled to achieve, everything was meaningless, a chasing after the wind; nothing was gained under the sun" (Eccles. 2:11). This narrative feels like the end of a great movie but with a sad and empty, gut-wrenching finality. Really, after all this, he's still not happy? What hope is there for us?

BECOME DISORIENTED

We live in an upside-down kingdom, and in order to find joy we have to become disoriented. That sounds crazy because in the human sense, when we become befuddled or confused we lose our way and may become disappointed or angry. Often when a plane or helicopter pilot flies in the fog or deep clouds and becomes disoriented, they cannot see the ground. In a helicopter, the pilot has no way of determining which direction is up until the vehicle moves at a speed where air resistance kicks in. But at that point it may be too late to rescue the situation. Some investigators suspect this happened to the helicopter that crashed near the Los Angeles suburb of Calabasas and killed the famous NBA legend 41-year old Kobe Bryant, his 13-year-old daughter, Giana, and seven others.

Why give you sad and confusing news that might throw you off course and harm you?

In order to invite joy, you have to become disoriented to the way the world functions. If you keep going on this crazy pathway to finding satisfaction, you're going to crash. You can't keep buying whatever you feel you want or deserve and maxing out your credit cards. How long can you keep up that insane pace at the workplace? How many years is it going to take before you forgive those who have hurt you? When will you stop being jealous of someone else's blessings and start being grateful for the life God has given you? When will you stop spending hours on your computer and phone and start spending time with the people who mean the most to you? You won't find joy in the crazy; you find joy in living the way of the upside-down kingdom. Here's how Jesus told us to do it:

- To get back at your enemy, love him (Matt. 5:43–44).
- Instead of looking for places of honour, humble yourself and let God lift you up (James 4:10).
- To become great, become a servant (Matt. 20:27–28).
- To truly find joyful life, die to self (Matt. 16:24–25).
- To become rich, give your money away (Luke 6:38).
- To find rest, walk with Jesus (Matt. 11:28).

In order to fill yourself up with joy, you have to do it the inverted way. You have to pour out. Pouring out forgiveness, humility, and sacrificial love is the first step to getting off the "crazy" path and walking in sync with Jesus. Time must be set aside not to go for the crazy but to seek Jesus's heart, which is gentle and humble and where you will find rest for your soul.

POUR OUT OR FILL UP

In February 2020, I was back in Colombia with Margaret Gibb and the Women Together Team, speaking at three CALLED conferences in three Colombian cities. One of the conferences was held in Bogota, a huge city of 11 million people where everyone is focused on getting to their destination at breakneck speed. The traffic is crazy. Oftentimes while our driver was weaving through traffic I shouted out, "Look, guys, he's driving down the white line!" "Oh my goodness, we almost hit that pedestrian." "He's going to hit that bus!" "Did you just see that motorcyclist weave between those cars?" It was impossible to hold back my emotions amid all the noise and speed, and I was afraid that someone was going to get killed. I needed to get off that crazy roller coaster ride.

No wonder Jesus went away to a mountaintop to intentionally seek calm and speak to his heavenly father. Mountaintops are serene and refreshing escapes where we see life from a different and calmer perspective.

Toward the end of our Colombian tour, outside of the rugged city limits of Bucaramanga, I got my mountaintop experience. Our team was scheduled to conduct discipleship training at the Yuventud Con Una Mision YWAM camp situated on the side of a mountain with a breathtaking view. The morning of our teaching, we were picked up at our hotel, and I buckled up for our adventure. After our vehicle spiralled up the highway toward the camp and then bounced over potholes and steep inclines, we arrived at the camp to the echoing sound of a guitar, tambourine, and Spanish worship songs. As the warm air and music swept over me, my body calmed, and I took in the majestic surroundings. The lush Amazon jungle spread over the mountains, and yet we took pictures of trees within arm's length that grew bananas, mangos, avocados, and limes. We were surrounded by the unimaginable splendour of lush vegetation and vibrant colourful flowers. Encompassed by beauty and music, I was overcome with emotion. I couldn't stop the tears. They were an overflow of the joy of our Father's multi-faceted and colourful creation and gifts. Heavenliness and joy are found in the calm.

After we finished our training session, we took the YWAM director's group leader, Jorge Parejo, for an ice cream treat at a famous Colombian restaurant called Crepes and Waffles. While we dug into our sumptuous ice cream creations, we talked about the Venezuelan refugee crisis and how over two million refugees had now entered Colombia. When I asked how the country and in particular Christians were dealing with this tinderbox, Jorge's face lit up, and he shared his story of the "Living Truth" tents set up at the Venezuelan border crossing of Cucuta. Jorge told us about his vision of setting up tents to feed and comfort the refugees and how God provided the finances, volunteers, and food to feed up to 500 people per day. His face lit up with joy when he told us about teams of volunteers coming in from Canada and the United States to feed the hungry and to comfort the broken-hearted. He told stories of miracle upon miracle and how they are able to share the Good News of Jesus Christ and even baptize some people in the nearby river. He went on to tell us how they held people in their arms and how some of them died days later. Even though all of it is hard, sacrificial, and dependent on God's strength and provision, Jorge's eyes were bright, and they gleamed with joy.

That's what pouring out does: it fills us up with unexplainable provisions. Jorge experienced joy because he was obeying the command to pour himself out and feed the hungry. The Bible says, "For I was hungry and you gave me something to eat, I was thirsty and you gave me something to drink, I was a stranger and you invited me in, I needed clothes and you clothed me, I was sick and you looked after me" (Matt. 25:35–36). You see, Jorge was joyful because he was flying upside down. He wasn't saying "What can the world do for me?" Instead he took the stance "What can I do for the world?"

That's what happens when we decide to spend time on a mountaintop. We take time to become calm and stop seeing the way the world functions. We settle in to learn the upside-down rhythms and examples of Jesus and become bold enough to act like him. Calm is our soul's love language. That's where we find truth and joy.

RETURN TO SANITY

Why do we run so hard? Have we confused productivity with activity? I believe that the desire to overwork is an attempt to establish our self-worth through our net worth. We want to be loved and admired, and so we overachieve, and our life gets crazy. Marcus Buckingham in his book *Find Your Strongest Life* tells us that busyness does not evoke joy. "Over the last forty years women have secured for themselves greater opportunity, greater achievement, greater influence, and more money. But over the same time period, they have become less happy, more anxious and more stressed; and in ever-increasing numbers, they are medicating themselves for it."[62]

We don't like disappointing people or upsetting anyone, and so we say "yes" to too many things. There is something wrong when we say yes for reasons that do not align with the desires and priorities of God's will for our lives. When we operate out of our weaknesses and lack of self-worth, the slightest demands have the power to intimidate us. We need to know how to establish God's design for our life by knowing when to say yes and when to say no. To return to sanity we have to learn to fly upside down and establish boundaries that align our life with God's best version of who we are becoming. Saundra Dalton-Smith in her book *Sacred Rest* describes it this way: "Boundaries are how you protect the fruitful areas of your life from becoming burned out, depleted, and exhausted. Every yes out of obligation is like a thief sneaking into your field eating away at the fruit of your life, each weakening you and making it harder to sustain the fullness you are capable of holding."[63]

Never underestimate the power and possibility of what a woman can do. If we put our mind to it we "could" do anything. After all, the Bible tells us, "I can do all this though him who gives me strength" (Phil. 4:13). But to return to sanity and live as joyful women

---

62. Marcus Buckingham, *Find Your Strongest Life: What the Happiest and Most Successful Women Do Differently* (Nashville: Thomas Nelson, 2009), 14.

63. Saundra Dalton-Smith, *Sacred Rest: Recover Your Life, Renew Your Energy, Restore Your Sanity* (New York: FaithWords, 2017), 127–128.

we need to know what God's best is for our life. Because the Bible also tells us, "All you need to say is simply 'Yes' or 'No'; anything beyond this comes from the evil one" (Matt. 5:37). Each opportunity that comes our way invites these questions: "God, is this the best for my life and my family? God, do I say yes or no? God, help me to find my best yes and guide me to claim my worth only in you."

The busiest and craziest time in a mother's life is during the child-rearing days, and it's often difficult to know when to say the fruitful yes and no. A dynamic woman whom I've been mentoring since she was 16, and who is now my goddaughter with a husband and three sons, has learned when to say yes and no and has established solid boundaries. Here is Cheryl's story:

How do we find joy during the busiest season of child-rearing? Life can be so chaotic and stressful that we often miss the little moments of joy. Learning when to say "yes" and "no" is a huge part of finding calm and joy.

I don't consider myself an expert on parenting, but as a mother of three boys, ages 15, 13, and 8, there are a few lessons I have learned along the way. Even though it sounds like a cliché, my number one lesson is to be organized. Sure, there are bumps along the way, but with laying out the boys' clothes the night before and keeping lunches and agendas up to date, life is calmer and easier. Get your children involved; they are quite capable of helping with the organization.

Lesson number two is to have a few good friends. Not a plethora of Facebook friends but a few close friends you can connect with by phone or face to face a few times a month. It's helpful and therapeutic for me to talk to someone at the same stage of life. We can cry or laugh about situations. My friends offer me comfort and encouragement to keep running the race of parenting. As mothers our job is not to be martyrs but to be the godliest parents and the best version of who God made us to be. That means taking time just for ourselves.

Lesson number three is to be present. That doesn't mean just showing up at ballet class or basketball games but to be present with your body language and mind. Because I have three boys involved in sports, you will often find me on a football field. I watch each game cheering and encouraging my children from the sidelines. I don't want to miss any plays by being fixated and busy on my phone as some other parents are prone to do. Even sadder is that some parents don't come at all. Being a part of whatever your child does, experiencing the highs and lows, will bring you joy. It will connect you with your child, and they will love you for it.

As a parent I make mistakes every day and don't always get it right. I do know this. I want to enjoy the ride and experience joy in the midst of all the chaos and busyness.[64]

I know that none of us want to come to the end of our productive years and end with the regretful words of King Solomon that "everything was meaningless." We'll never find lasting joy in the hairpin turns and speed on the super highways. Sure, it may give a momentary jolt of fun and thrill, but that will quickly fade, and we're off looking for the next thrill. Which whiteboard words do you want to incorporate into your life? "Calm" or "Crazy"? It's your daily choice.

GROW YOUR JOY

1. Go crazy with some fun. There are times for craziness. I'm absolutely crazy about my grandchildren and have been known to do some zany things. In 2018 it was time to teach them how to blow bubbles with Hubba Bubba gum. After buying big packages of gum, I taught them how to chew the gum until it was just the right consistency and then how to blow bubbles. It wasn't easy. We had to resort to watching gum blowing on YouTube and practising in front of the mirror. And finally the fun began when we had a competition to see who could blow the biggest bubbles. What memories! What laughter! It's good for you. "A cheerful heart is good medicine, but a crushed spirit dries up the bones" (Prov. 17:22).

2. Be aware of burnout. Running hard, being over ambitious, and not knowing when to say yes and no will lead to burnout, and it will feel like you're falling off a cliff. Carey Nieuwhof in his book *Didn't See It Coming* gives a raw glimpse into his descent into burnout.

> Over a period of years, I had come to realize that so much of my interior life was skewed … there was an abundance of insecurity, jealousy, and fear and a deep misunderstanding of identity and fulfillment. I began to realize that at some point in my childhood, I'd concluded that love was earned by performance. The better I did, the more loved I would be … The more people I meet and the more I look around our culture, the more I think there may be many people suffering from burnout or what I might call "low-grade burnout." By that I mean the joy of life is gone, but the functions of life continue. You're not dead, but you're certainly not feeling fully alive.[65]

I wonder if these words wreck your heart as they do mine. We can't keep running hard and crazy without expecting to crash. It's time to go against the grain and climb

---

64. Used with permission from Cheryl Klippenstein.

65 Nieuwhof, *Didn't See It Coming*, 146, 150.

that mountaintop. It's not always easy to stop the perpetual motion and soak in God's presence and be thankful for all you have. But you must come to the conclusion you don't need more. What you have is enough. "In him our hearts rejoice, for we trust in his holy name" (Ps. 33:21).

3. Let go of control. For a trapeze artist to be successful, there needs to come a time when he or she lets go of the ropes. Now is your time to let go of the world's demands and trust God to provide and look after you. Matthew 10:39 says, "Whoever finds their life will lose it, and whoever loses their life for my sake will find it." Surrendering your time and life to God is moving him back into his position as Lord of your life. There are many distractions and idols fighting for your heart and weighing you down with all the clutter. When will you live unattached to the validation of others and come boldly into the place of freedom and joy? Can you pull away to rest and become calm and still trust God to provide all your needs? When will you stop justifying all that you do to prove your self-worth? Letting go and trusting God is hard, but it's the only way to the pathway of joy. May you be able to say, "I trust in your unfailing love; my heart rejoices in your salvation" (Ps. 13:5).

4. Keep calm and carry on. These are the words on a motivational poster produced by the British government in 1939 in preparation for World War II. The poster was intended to raise the morale of the British public threatened with widely predicted mass air attacks on major cities. You have to recognize that your present war is against busyness, distractions, too many demands, and believing the lies of the enemy that you need to do it all. You can't change the world around you, but you can change your focus and priorities. May God help you to find your calm so that you can boldly declare, "May my meditation be pleasing to him, as I rejoice in the LORD" (Ps. 104:34).

AND ASK GOD TO MAKE YOU JOYFUL

Ask God, What needs to change in my life so that I can continually experience the calm and joy of a mountaintop experience?

S—Scripture: "This is the day the LORD has made. We will rejoice and be glad in it" (Ps. 118:24).

T—Thanksgiving: Thank you, God, for each new day brimming with life and new hope. Everything you make is good, so I thank you in advance for the goodness of each day. I know I have the ability to rejoice, and because of your spirit you can guide and teach me how to find this constant flow of joy. Thank you that you have created astounding mountaintop experiences where I can rejoice in your abundant goodness.

O—Observation: In spite of my unreliable feelings and the craziness of my circumstances, I know I can still rejoice. Some days it just feels too hard. I can't do this on my own, and I need to create my own mountaintop experiences. I know I need those places of calm, whether it's in a quiet spot in my home or in the beauty of creation. This won't happen on its own, and I must intentionally get out of the fast lane to pursue the joy available to me.

P—Prayer: God, I'm so thankful that you do not condemn me, because I can do a pretty good job of condemning myself. I try so hard to do what's right but encounter many distractions throughout the day. I receive your promise: "Remain in my love. If you keep my commands, you will remain in my love, just as I have kept my Father's commands and remain in his love. I have told you this so that my joy may be in you and that your joy may be complete" (John 15:9–11). Father, help me find those calm places where I can settle in and learn how to remain in your love. I want the fullness and pleasure of experiencing your joy in spite of what life throws at me. I know it's available to me; please take my hand and lead me to your mountain. Thank you. Amen.

JOYFUL WHISPERS
HEARING GOD'S VOICE

"God often speaks loudest when we're the quietest."
—Mark Batterson[66]

Sitting alone and frightened in my little white Jetta, I turned the ignition key one more time. Nothing. My car was dead. I was stranded in the parking lot outside the Holiday Inn in Portland, Oregon, and still had a five-hour drive to the retreat centre where I was the keynote speaker. The day before, my faithful vehicle had performed perfectly for the entire twelve-hour road trip from my home in Kelowna, British Columbia, to the outskirts of Portland, Oregon. But right now I wasn't going anywhere and didn't even know where to turn for help.

Dead silence mocked me each time I turned the key. On the dashboard red letters warned me that I had a dead battery and engine failure. Anxious thoughts swirled in my mind: *Come on, Heidi, don't panic; there has to be a solution. What happened? Did I leave lights on in my car last night? Maybe someone in the hotel knows who to call. Will my BCAA membership work here? How will I get to the retreat centre in time? Oh my goodness, this is awful. God, why is this happening?*

After I took several deep breaths, my mind calmed, and I began to pray. "God, you know I'm being obedient, driving all this way to share your love and promises to women

---

66. Mark Batterson, *Whisper: How to Hear the Voice of God* (New York: Crown Publishing Group, 2017), 212.

at a Sand to Pearls retreat. I'm stuck. You have to help me. Please show me what to do so I can get back on the road."

Within seconds I heard God whisper to me, "Turn the key one more time."

Really, God? I already did that several times.

Again God prompted me: "Turn the key one more time."

So I did. I was thrilled with delight as the car sprang to life. Within seconds, I was back on Highway I-5 heading toward Bend, Oregon. Singing and praising God, I began the final phase of my trip. Finally, I was able to enjoy the lush and exquisite Oregon scenery and vegetation. God had whispered my miracle, and my heart overflowed with joy.

Over the next four hours, I had ample time to think and reflect on how often, since Jack's death, I had heard God's voice. While I was married to Jack, Jack was my voice of wisdom and guidance, and I loved listening to him with my ears. But now that I'm on my own and God is my husband, I've had to learn to listen to God's whispers with my heart. Like a baby learning to understand a parent's voice, I'm hearing God speak to me in magnificent and strange ways and places. Through this process, I'm discovering that God is as close as the breath we breathe, and like a father with his children, he desires deep intimacy and an honest relationship.

THE INTIMACY OF A WHISPER

In order to hear someone's whisper, we have to lean in and pay attention. To whisper is to speak very softly, using one's breath without one's vocal cords. To hear God's breath, I have to get radically close because that's where he wants me. It's not easy to find stillness in our present culture that thrives on constant distractions and living out loud. Strangely enough, though, we're not the only generation to struggle with silence and proactive listening. I was startled when I read this quote from French philosopher Blaise Pascal, who died in 1662: "The sole cause of man's unhappiness is that he does not know how to stay quietly in his room." Really? I can't imagine busyness and distractions during that time of history. To unleash joy we must battle against all intrusions. The only way to know God and hear his voice is to "Be still, and know that I am God" (Ps. 46:10). How do we do that?

Stop the busyness.

Turn down the noise.

Become still.

Listen for his whispers.

Until we learn to live in quiet, intimate harmony and voiceless community with God, we won't hear the wooing of his whisper. I know we try in the midst of noisy traffic, blaring TVs, and the constant ping of phone notifications. Sadly, we are motivated and shaped by the loudest voices in our lives, and God's whispers get lost in the clamour. Which voice do you listen to the most?

The prophet Elijah also couldn't find God in the noise. After Elijah and his men killed 450 Baal worshippers and Elijah ran into the desert to escape the wrath of Queen Jezebel, he sat under a broom tree and prayed that he might die. "'I have had enough, LORD,' he said. 'Take my life'" (1 Kings 19:4 NLT). Then Elijah lay under the broom tree and fell asleep. Soon after, God's angel fed him. After a time of resting and renewal, Elijah travelled for 40 days and 40 nights to meet with God on Mount Horeb.

Elijah was to stand on the mountain as the Lord was about to pass by. Elijah thought he would find God in a windstorm, an earthquake, and a fire, but God was not in any of them. Then Elijah heard a gentle whisper. He pulled his cloak over his face, stepped out of his cave, and met with God. Finally, in the stillness, Elijah listened with a soft and open heart and was able to dialogue openly and honestly with God.

In God's whispers, we find truth and how to take our next steps. The truth is, Elijah was not the only one zealous for serving the Lord; there were 7,000 in Israel whose knees had not bowed down to Baal. The next step for Elijah was to "Go back the way you came" (1 Kings 19:15) and anoint other kings and his successor: Elisha, son of Shaphat. Through stillness and uprightness, Elijah's troubled heart heard God, and Elijah knew his next steps.

Our focus should not be on using God's whispers just for information. Prioritizing an intimate relationship with God gets us everything we need, including next steps. Everything he says to us comes from a heart of deep, intense love. Chris Tiegreen in his devotional book *Hearing His Voice* understands this so clearly: "The more we build that relationship, being sensitive to the ways He moves and the thoughts He fills us with, the more we will be able to hear God's words in any given situation."[67]

I'm so grateful I stopped to hear God tell me to "turn the car key one more time." Those words were a gift that changed the trajectory of my day, got me to the retreat centre on time, and moved me into inexpressible joy.

NOT "ONE SIZE FITS ALL"

God speaks to us in many ways but mostly through his word. He also speaks through other people, music, nature, dreams, and visions. There is not a "one size fits all" way God speaks. Throughout the Bible, God spoke through a burning bush, a donkey, a dove, writing on the wall, a fleece, and in an audible voice. God also speaks to us through other people's teaching, preaching, and prophesying.

I love how God speaks to me when I ask him questions. I learned this new discipline through a course offered by my home church, Trinity Church Kelowna. They used the *Hearing God* manual created by Southland Church in Steinbach, Manitoba, Canada.

67. Tiegreen, *Hearing His Voice Devotional*, 9.

I'd never before thought to ask God a question and then, with pen poised, wait for his answers. This discipline of listening for God's voice and writing down his answers opened up a whole new God dimension for me. At first I grappled with the answers, thinking, *Is this my voice or God's? What if I'm making this up? Is it my own conscience through learned behaviour? How can I tell the difference?* I wondered the same way Mark Batterson did in his book *Whisper* and how he challenged himself with "We don't always hear what's actually being said. Why? Because we hear everything through the filter of our histories, our personalities, our ethnicities, and our theologies."[68] Yes, initially it's confusing, but over time the process becomes exciting as God's voice, spoken into our spirits through the Holy Spirit, brings words and pictures into order.

God's Spirit has been at work since creation, hovering over the earth and bringing chaos into order. Separating a formless mass of darkness and creating light. Separating waters and creating dry ground and seed-bearing plants (Gen. 1:1–11). That Spirit now lives within us to help separate truth from lies and whispers, to change our frustrations and disappointments into joy and divine appointments. When we don't hear him, he's not snubbing us; he's waiting for us to draw closer. Those who know God best will hear the clearest and loudest. In fact, the more we lean into his whispers, the louder his words become, like a megaphone that sifts through the clutter of other thoughts and amplifies the volume of God's voice. God knows our personalities and will get our attention in unique ways only you and I can understand.

It can be in the feeling of a burning in our spirit to awaken our soul to listen. Remember the story of the disciples walking with Jesus from Jerusalem to Emmaus after Jesus rose from the dead? Jesus was right there walking and talking with them, but in those moments, they didn't recognize him or his voice. Then something quickened their spirits, their eyes were opened, and they exclaimed, "Were not our hearts burning within us while he talked with us on the road and opened the Scriptures to us?" (Luke 24:32). Jesus's words and presence were like a flame burning in their spirits.

Don't be afraid to ask God questions and wait for his answers, which can come through a burning in your spirit, an imprint of words that just won't go away, or a megaphone voice that is louder than all the rest. Over the years, I've had God speak to me through a word on a billboard, a phrase on a coffee cup, a magazine article, a Facebook post, and so many other ways that my listing them would begin to bore you!

Never limit the way God speaks to us.

ANSWERS IN THE WHISPERS

The *Hearing God* module became my inspiration and the starting point for me to ask God questions and bravely write down his answers. After six weeks of intensive

---

68. Batterson, *Whisper*, 28.

studying and journaling, I was no longer afraid to have my pen poised and ready to write down God's answers to my questions. I like to keep it simple so it doesn't become too cumbersome and I end up quitting. Here are two of my favourite exercises to hear God's voice.

1. Read a Bible passage and ask God to reveal **one thing** he wants to teach you. Use the S.T.O.P. method I use at the end of each chapter in this book. To date, I've gone through the Gospel of John, the psalms, and parts of Isaiah, and with each reading I ask, "God, what do you want to teach me today?" The results and answers are life altering.

2. Ask God any question. Then with an open heart and pen in hand begin the conversation between you and God. The following is an unedited version of dialogue that took place after I asked God a raw and vulnerable question on August 31, 2018.

> Heidi: God, what do you see when you look at me?
>
> God: Someone trying to live a "good life."
>
> Heidi: Yes, I am trying. After all these years, why am I still so hard on myself?
>
> God: You still compare yourself to the world's and people's standards.
>
> Heidi: I agree, I do, and most often I come up short, in my writing, speaking, and golf. My golf game sucks right now; why?
>
> God: Your striving is stiffening your soul and your body. Relax and remain in me and simply enjoy how I've made you.
>
> Heidi: I'm still human. I live in a harsh and competitive world. Some days are filled with inadequacies and struggles.
>
> God: Come to me. Compare yourself to me. My yoke is easy and my burden is light. Learn to walk in my acceptance and love. Work on your love and not striving and comparing.
>
> Heidi: I do try very hard. Help me to lean in and find my strength and myself in you and who you made me to be. Help me to accept myself and relax in who I am. Weaknesses, failures, and all.
>
> God: I am with you and involved in every area of your life. Come to me. Let me help you.
>
> Heidi: Thank you. I will.

Looking back at my words I know they came from God through the Holy Spirit. On my own I would never use the words "Your striving is stiffening your soul and your body."

I listened with my soul, and those words from the Holy Spirit were profound, and I took them to heart. Over the next while, I loosened up and gave myself more grace. Even my golf game improved.

I think it's wonderful that we live in a society where we want our voice to be heard. But sadly, instead of leaning in and listening with an open heart, many people are too busy preparing their story and response. We're not fully engaged. Five times in the Bible there is a variation of Jesus's words "Whoever has ears to hear, let them hear" (Mark 4:9; Matt. 11:15, 13:9; Rev. 2:29, 3:22). Jesus is saying, "Don't let things go into one ear and out of the other. Listen with your whole heart and soul; I want to tell you something important." God, who parted the Red Sea and walked on water, knows you better than you know yourself. To find joy you have to get close enough to hear his whispers of who you are and let him help you discover your glorious life. So go ahead, get out of the box, get your pen and paper, and ask God some radical questions.

- God, I know you love me, but do you like me?
- What would you like me to begin doing in my life? What steps should I take to start this?
- Do I spend my money wisely?
- What barriers are stopping me from experiencing fresh joy?
- Have I hurt anyone lately?
- How can I be a better spouse, friend, or sibling?

God directs our steps even if we think we're the one taking them. His voice becomes clear to those who take the time to listen, so let his whispers awaken your spirits and make you come alive and joyful.

Chris Tiegreen tells us how to approach this process. "Approach the listening process with a commitment to do whatever God says. He doesn't want us to hear His voice as an option to consider. He wants us to hear Him as the absolute truth. When we come with a commitment to believe what He says, He is much more eager to speak."[69] God uses the language of our hearts to give us daily purpose and make our life meaningful.

OUR WHISPERING PLACE

Finding our whispering place takes intentionality and creativity. Why? Because it needs to be a spot set aside that we can run to and where there are no distractions, ideally a sacred place surrounded in loveliness that gives us joy and comfort.

I have two whispering places. My favourite is my armchair, with navy, turquoise, and green leaves, beside my fireplace. Here I'm surrounded with the pleasure and serenity of family photos and colourful pillows. All around me are decor signs that say "BLESSED,"

---

69. Tiegreen, *Hearing His Voice Devotional*, 127.

"THANKFUL," "UNSTOPPABLE," and "CALLED," and they inspire me to be attentive and praise God. My second favourite is a five-kilometre walk along vineyards, lakes, and mountains where God shows off his greatest majesty. It's in those "be still" places that I can dial in to let God's voice be a pathway to something great.

But we're not limited to defined places. Throughout the Old and New Testament God spoke to people in various ways and places.

- To Mary through an angel who promised the birth of Jesus (Luke 1:26–38)
- To Joseph while he was in prison, where God helped Joseph to interpret dreams (Gen. 41:25–36)
- To Moses through a burning bush (Exod. 3)
- To Hannah through a priest at God's house (1 Sam. 1:9–15)
- To Elijah on Mount Horeb (1 Kings 19:9–18)
- To King Belshazzar through the fingers of a human hand writing on the wall of the king's palace (Dan. 5:5)
- To Ruth through the wisdom of her mother-in-law, Naomi (Ruth 3:1–4)
- To Balaam through his donkey (Num. 22:28)

Today God's Spirit lives within us and can meet us any place at any time. The following is a story from my friend Carol Rath, who in the midst of pain found her whispering place in her mother's arms.

I'm a joyful person, but that doesn't mean I've never suffered heartache or pain. In fact, there was a dark and devastating period in my life when I no longer wanted to live.

I had just turned 42, and life couldn't have gotten any better. I was living the dream, with a fantastic job, my dream home, and my perfect family. I was married to my high school sweetheart and financially secure, and our teenaged son and two daughters were actively involved in our local church. Life had arrived and was exactly how I had always hoped and dreamed it would be.

But I was unprepared for the devastating declaration "I don't love you anymore." The perfect world that I'd devoted 20 years of my life to creating deflated like a punctured balloon in less than five minutes. Nothing could have prepared me for my overwhelming devastation when my husband informed me he was leaving me and pursuing a relationship with a woman 15 years my junior.

God in his mercy blessed me with a very wise and loving mother. Somehow I managed to gather my wounded broken self and get to her home. As I crouched by her rocking chair she didn't say a word but gathered me into her arms, pressed her face into my ear, and softly sang the words to an old gospel hymn: "Turn your eyes upon Jesus, look full in his wonderful face; and the things of life will grow strangely dim, in the light of his glory and grace." Those words and that tender touch were like a healing balm to my ravaged being and were to become a defining moment in my life. As she sang, I raised my head and looked heavenward, and in that moment of being in God's presence I experienced a miracle of love and grace. Brokenness and despair gave way to joy and peace as God's fresh joy flooded my wounded soul, and in that moment I knew everything would be okay.

Over the years God has spoken to me in different ways. My mother taught me to memorize the Scriptures and, whenever things got tough, to look up and claim the promises in the Bible. Throughout the years, God's whispers have provided a way where there seemed to be no way. His blessings have far surpassed anything I could have ever asked for or imagined. I constantly remind myself that the short dash between the two dates on a headstone is not a destination but a journey. Like all journeys, it will be filled with bumps, detours, and devastating crashes in the form of heartache, loss, and disappointment. As long as we make an active choice to find our whispering place and turn our eyes upon Jesus and in all things give thanks, he will fill us with unspeakable joy.[70]

Learning to hear God's whispers has opened a new world of understanding. God wants to talk to us so he can guide us into our best and joyful life. Thousands of years ago, God used Isaiah to prompt his people to "Come to me with your ears wide open. Listen, and you will find life" (Isa. 55:3 TLB).

Let's learn to listen with a soft and open heart, understanding that God always leads us toward wholeness and joy.

GROW YOUR JOY

1. Ask God for two words. For 19 years, in the month of January I've always gone for a long walk and asked God to give me two words for the coming year. Sounds too simple, right? However, my focusing on two words, studying them, and soaking in them has allowed the Holy Spirit to embed truths and joy into my spirit in exceptionally surprising ways. In 2006, one of my words was *small*, and I wondered what God would want to teach me about such a nonessential word. By the end of that year, the word *small* had shifted my perspective on how God sees the world and how I see it. As a speaker and author, I'm looking for the "big," but God does his greatest work through the small and seemingly insignificant acts of love and kindness.

---

70. Used with permission from Carol Rath.

After we live with a word or two for a whole year, it gets embedded into our spirit and transforms our thinking and the way we live and see life. In 2017, the year after Jack died, my two words were *hope* and *healing*. To unpack those words, I bought books on hope and healing, I studied Bible verses, I blogged, I asked questions, and I prayed for God to unleash hope and healing in my life. Those words became the lenses through which God revealed to me that he is a God who gives us hope and heals. By the end of 2017, hope and healing had grown roots into my spirit, and I know for certain they escalated the unleashing of joy.

2. Create your own S.T.O.P. method. I need to do things that are practical and work. In 2006, I asked God for a simple but meaningful method to help me understand and live out his words. I'm a high-energy mission-focused woman, and one day, in the midst of my whirling, I heard God say, "Heidi, *stop* and listen."

Jesus knows how confused, distracted, and busy we are, and we need to stop and wait for him to speak. This led me to create my own S.T.O.P. method.

To see if this method would inspire intimacy with God, I invited a group of women to come with their Bibles, papers, and pens and meet me at one of our city parks. I told them to find a lovely spot under a tree, read Ephesians 1 at least three times, and ask the Holy Spirit to illuminate one verse that was meant just for them. I asked them to follow the S.T.O.P. acronym. After 40 minutes, they came back, we sat in a circle, and each woman read what God had revealed to them. As they shared their verses, explained their observations, and read their prayers, I witnessed something spectacular. God had revealed himself to them in a profound way, and they experienced joy. That's what happens when we stop to read God's Word, wait to hear from him, and enjoy his presence and his whispers. Joy shows up.

3. Walk and listen. Jesus knows how confused and busy we are. I think we're like lost sheep, and that's why he gave us an illustration about shepherds and sheep. We need to learn to recognize the voice of our shepherd so that when he calls us, even in the midst of a multitude of other voices, we recognize and have a "knowing" of his distinctive sound. He wants us to know him so intimately that in all of our experiences of feelings, smells, and sounds we will know it is him. He tells us, "My sheep listen to my voice; I know them, and they follow me" (John 10:27).

On November 19 of 2018, I decided to do something radical to hear God's voice through the sights, smells, and sounds of his creation. For five months I went for five-kilometre walks and asked God this question: "God, what do you want to tell me today?" As I heard God's voice speak to me through my thoughts and impressions, I quickly recorded the unedited words on my cellphone. As soon as I walked through the doors of my home, I quickly entered the words into my computer. After five months, I had over 20 pages of single-spaced notes. I am still amazed at how profoundly simple his answers were and how our ongoing conversations unleashed deep insights into his character. All his answers pointed to smells, sounds, and images in his creation. For example,

- On December 1, 2018, as I walked by a row of rose bushes that still had rosehip seeds on them, God's words came to me: "Everything starts with a seed." Then more words came about how joy is a seed within us that we need to nurture and grow.
- December 3, 2018, was a cold and windy day. God's words to me that day were "I am the wind of the Spirit." This was an incredibly powerful conversation about how his spirit is like the wind. We cannot see it, grab it, or harness it, but it is always there and moving.
- January 12, 2019, was a dreary day. It was three in the afternoon, and as I walked through the vineyards there was still fog that hid many trees and the mystical landscape. Then I heard God say, "I am the vine." To find clarity and stay connected to him I needed to come out of my own fog so that God could make my life clear and purposeful.
- On February 5, 2019, he told me, "There are treasures in the darkness." Then on March 4, he said, "In your distress come to the mercy seat." On March 18, God told me, "I am the God who was, is, and is to come." After each of my questions, God gently and brilliantly met me in all my senses and gave me answers that often blew my mind. Most of these walks took place in the winter months in Canada, and often when I arrived home I would throw off my winter gear, run to my computer, and eagerly rewrite his answers. Often, I couldn't type fast enough as awe and joy erupted from my soul.

I highly encourage you to try this at home. It will help you to discern God's voice above all the other noises and distractions, and I can assure you that you will discover things you never knew. Including renewed joy.

4. Answer Jesus's question. In the story of Bartimaeus, the blind beggar was begging Jesus to help him. Twice Bartimaeus called out to Jesus to heal him: "Son of David, have mercy on me." Of course, Jesus knew Bartimaeus was blind and needed healing, but still Jesus asked him, "What do you want me to do for you?" (Mark 10:47–51). After the blind beggar told Jesus he wanted to see, Jesus healed him. I believe with all my heart that this question is for all of us. To grow our joy, we need to ask Jesus to give it to us. I don't fully understand this. Jesus knows we need it, but still he wants us to ask. So let's ask. Ask Jesus to help you tap into the currency of heaven, to help you know and experience fresh joy.

AND ASK GOD TO MAKE YOU JOYFUL

Ask God, How do I lean in to hear your voice?

S—Scripture: "Be still, and know that I am God" (Ps. 46:10).

T—Thanksgiving: God, I stand in awe of your majesty, beauty, and power. And yet you want to meet with me, a mere mortal, to tell me great and marvellous things. Thank you that you value me enough to share your truths and glorious insights. Thank you that through impossible situations you are right there to whisper solutions and my next steps. Thank you that you will teach me to hear your whispers in ways that I can understand.

O—Observation: Is it really possible that God will speak to me? I believe it for other people, but is it also true for me? I don't fully understand how this works, but with all my heart I want to hear God's voice. I want God to give me pictures and insights to prepare me for each day and lead me into my best future. I need to know how to draw close to God so that I can hear his whispers. I hunger for the joy that comes from being deeply connected to God.

P—Prayer: God, first of all, forgive me for using you as my source of information instead of seeking your heart. I truly do hunger for your love, truth, and joy. Please remove my distorted perceptions of how you speak to people and show me how to lean in to hear your whispers. Thank you for teaching dull ears such as mine. I long to have you pour your whispers into my soul like a spiritual injection. Help me to cut through all the other voices and distractions so that I can develop my confidence in knowing when it is your voice. Draw me close so that I don't just hear your words but I can hear your heart. God, keep my gaze upon you. Impart your nature and heartbeat within me so that I can experience fresh joy. Thank you. Amen.

EPILOGUE

It is my greatest desire that you find the fresh joy that God designed all of us to have. Joy is a fruit of the Spirit that is received when we begin our relationship with Jesus Christ. This beautiful and unshakable joy is rooted in God and is available to all of us at any time, in any circumstance. Receiving this free and life-changing spiritual gift starts with taking a step to receive Jesus Christ as your personal saviour.

You start this relationship with our Holy God by praying and asking Jesus, the Son of God, to forgive you from all your past sins. All the bad things you have done in your life have negative power over you and keep you on a treadmill of seeking fleeting happiness. But when you confess your sins to God, he forgives every one of them. The Bible promises, "if we confess our sins to him, he can be depended on to forgive us and to cleanse us from every wrong" (1 John 1:9 TLB). What would that prayer do? It would reconnect you back to your creator, God. Pray this simple prayer with me.

Father,

You loved the world so much you gave your only begotten son to die for my sins so that I will not perish but have everlasting life. I believe and confess with my mouth that Jesus Christ is your son, the saviour of the world. I believe he died on the cross for me and bore all my sins, paying the price for them. I acknowledge that I have sinned, and I ask you to please forgive me for my sins. Fill me with the Holy Spirit and give me the gift of eternal life. Be my power by giving me the mind of Christ to help me on the pathway to embracing the glorious and fulfilling life you created for me. Fill me with your joy.

Thank you that you will. Amen.

Now that God has forgiven all your sins, you must turn around and forgive everyone who has hurt you. This is not an option—the Bible commands us to forgive. "Be gentle and ready to forgive; never hold grudges. Remember, the Lord forgave you, so you must forgive others" (Col. 3:13 TLB).

I tell you in all sincerity that forgiving everyone in my life has set me free from all the hooks of shame, guilt, anger, and resentment and has unleashed this unexplainable joy. I know I will be in this transformation process for the rest of my life, but daily God is refilling me with the life-changing fruit of the Spirit of love, joy, peace, patience, and all the other qualities that saturate my soul with fulfillment. I want you to know this joy as well.

When I walk people through forgiveness, I use the following steps. In order to do a complete supernatural heart work, I suggest you go through all of them with each person whom you need to forgive.

1. On a sheet of paper write down the names of the people who have hurt or offended you.
2. Face the hurt and the hate. Write down how you feel about these people and their offences.
3. Acknowledge that Jesus died for your sins.
4. Decide that you will bear the burden of each person's sin. All true forgiveness is substitutionary, as Christ's forgiveness of us was.
5. Decide to forgive. Forgiveness is a conscious choice to let the other person off the hook and free yourself from the past. The feelings of freedom will eventually follow.
6. Take your list to God and pray, "God, I choose to forgive [name] for [list of offences, what they did, and how they made you feel]."
7. Destroy the list. You are now free.
8. Let go of expectations that your forgiveness will result in major changes in the other person.
9. Try to understand the people you have forgiven. They are also victims.
10. Expect positive results of forgiveness in yourself. In time, you will be able to think about the people who have offended you without hurt, anger, or resentment.
11. Thank God for the lessons you have learned and for setting you free.
12. Be sure to accept your part of the blame for the offences you suffered.
13. Do something to bless the person who hurt you.

Forgiveness is hard, and feelings of joy and freedom may take longer than you think. Please persevere. If someone hurt you deeply, it may take many prayers until the ugly hook is completely released from your heart. One day, you will be able to look that person in the eye and bless them. Then you will know you've experienced the powerful transformation from struggling to create your ideal life to living with refreshing joy.[71]

---

71. For a full discussion of these steps, see Heidi McLaughlin, *Sand to Pearls: Making Bold Choices to Enrich Your Life* (Sisters: Deep River Books, 2010), 230–231.

CASTLE QUAY BOOKS

ALL OF OUR AWARD WINNING BOOKS
ARE AVAILABLE AT
WWW.CASTLEQUAYBOOKS.COM

Sandee Macgregor

A Mother-Daughter
Devotional and
Shared Journal
Experience for
Psalm 119

"Girls desire to know they are beautiful and special. In a generation where outward beauty is adored and applauded on social media, we must be careful to help our daughters build their self worth on God's truths. I wish I'd had this book during my daughter's informative years whilst she was discovering her fragile identity. Through her finely crafted words, Sandee MacGregor takes mothers and daughters by the hand and awakens the truths in Psalm 119. Through building foundational biblical truths, she helps the reader craft beautiful and lasting heart connection mother-daughter relationships. This book needs to be lovingly pressed into the hand of every mother who is raising a daughter."

—**Heidi McLaughlin**, International speaker and author of *Fresh Joy: Finding Joy in the Midst of Loss, Hardship, and Suffering* (Castle Quay Books)

Study Psalm 119 with your daughter (8-year-olds and older) through guided questions, prayers, and journaling. Devotional topics relate Psalm 119 to friendship, serving others, showing love to others, overcoming hard times, compassion, and more. Also, throughout the devotional you'll discover fun bonding activity ideas to do together!

We want to partner with what God is doing in our world today and reach the full uninhibited potential of Christ's church!

Mary-Elsie Wolfe offers us a vision for leadership that is leading-edge yet moderate, traditional yet progressive. Drawing upon key Bible stories of women in Jesus' day, she looks at the prominence of women in the early church and then applies key principles in an effective way for our day, enlarging our view of the future as believers.

If we want to lead like Jesus, as Jesus defines leadership for us, we must apply these foundational leadership principles to our times while still wrapping everything in the truth of the love of God for his people and his work.

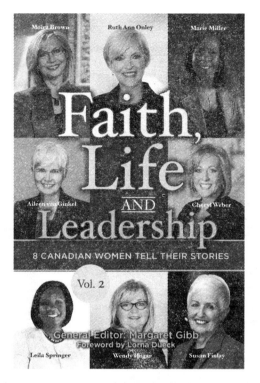

"Each one of these unique, personal, and vulnerable stories points to a bigger story: God's powerful story of calling, redemption, faithfulness, healing, provision, protection, and impact. You can't help being encouraged."
—**Dr. Steve Brown**, president of Arrow Leadership, author of *Leading Me*

"What makes this book compelling reading is to see and marvel at how God can take the raw materials of our lives—strengths, weaknesses, accomplishments, and failings—and fashion something beautiful and fruitful beyond our imagining."
—**Janet Clark**, PhD, senior VP Academic, Tyndale University College and Seminary

"As you discover these women, you will discover too how God has been working with your life for the good works prepared for you. Settle in for a good curious journey with the remarkable women in these pages."
—**Lorna Dueck**, CEO of Crossroads Christian Communications and YES TV

CASTLE QUAY BOOKS

"Get this book not only for yourself, but buy copies for your friends. It may just save their life. This is real!"—**Barbara Yoder**, apostle, Shekinah, Ann Arbor, MI

"*Because God Was There* will take you deep into the spiritual realm. This book should be in every counsellor's office."—**Moira Brown**, TV and radio personality

"What a story! This book should be turned into a movie."
—**Steve and Sandra Long**, senior leaders, Catch the Fire, Toronto

"A manual to lead you from tragedy to triumph."
—**Barry Maracle** (Mohawk), Desert Stream Ministries

"A must-read for every person who has ever experienced trauma or hurts in life, especially Indian residential/boarding school survivors."
—**Dr. Gerard and Peta-Gay Roberts**

"This down-to-earth book will bring hope, encouragement and fresh vision."
—**Mary Audrey Raycroft**, international speaker